THE ART OF

the

PERSONAL LETTER

Margaret Shepherd
with Sharon Hogan

BROADWAY BOOKS

New York

THE ART OF
the
PERSONAL LETTER

A Guide to Connecting Through
the Written Word

PUBLISHED BY BROADWAY BOOKS

Published in the United States by Broadway Books,
an imprint of The Doubleday Publishing Group,
a division of Random House, Inc., New York.
www.broadwaybooks.com

BROADWAY BOOKS and its logo, a letter B bisected on the diagonal,
are trademarks of Random House, Inc.

Book design by Nicola Ferguson

Library of Congress Cataloging-in-Publication Data

Shepherd, Margaret.
The art of the personal letter : a guide to connecting through the written
word / by Margaret Shepherd ; with Sharon Hogan.—1st ed.
            p.   cm.
1. Letter writing. 2. Letter writing—Social aspects. 3. Written
communication—Social aspects. I. Hogan, Sharon. II. Title.

PE1483.S426 2008

808.6—dc22   2008007237

ISBN 978-0-7679-2827-4

PRINTED IN THE UNITED STATES OF AMERICA

1   3   5   7   9   10   8   6   4   2

First Edition

To MY MOTHER,

Eleanor M. Shepherd

WHOSE LETTERS STILL SPEAK

TO ME.

The tongue is prone to lose the way,

Not so the pen, for in a letter

We have not better things to say,

But surely say them better.

—RALPH WALDO EMERSON, *"Life,"* 1847

CONTENTS

Contents

MARGARET SHEPHERD

September 1, 08
Boston

Dear Reader,

I'm so glad you're interested in personal letters! I know you'll enjoy getting acquainted with this wonderful art and then writing to the people you care about. It's a supremely simple and satisfying art that will survive and endure, in forms we can't even imagine yet, as long as people like you put it to use in their lives.

Authors write books for the same reasons people write letters. I write because I have something that I want to share, because writing to you helps me clarify my own thoughts, and because what connects all of us makes a difference to each of us, and to the world. Enjoy.

Yours

Margaret

ACKNOWLEDGMENTS

etter writers of all kinds—from my role models and lifelong correspondents to my fellow pack rats and sounding boards—have helped me put this book together. I want to thank Marilyn Brandt, Fred Fiske, Janet Fiske, Winifred Kelley, Michael Cann, Frank Randall, Lily Friend, Floyd Bradley, John LeGates, Swami Kumaresan, Stan Kugell, Lorraine Fricker, Stephanie Lukes, Susan Hackley, Zak Johnson, Gail Bernstein, Geoffrey Shepherd, Grethe Shepherd, Brooke Shearer, Patty O'Toole, Roberta Zonghi, C. D. Collins, Society of Printers members Lance Hidy, Booth Simpson, Dan Craven, and Steve Logowitz, *Writing Equipment Society Journal* editor Mike West, Ken Morse at MIT, Jodi Smith of Mannersmith, and my childhood friends Tara McConnell and Mark Peterson. Letters and advice from these people, and many more, have helped me understand where the art of letter writing might be headed.

My thanks go also to the helpful staff at the Biblioteks Vagten in Copenhagen, the Houghton and Schlesinger libraries at Harvard University, the Detroit Public Library, and the Boston Public Library.

I am grateful to Derrick Purser for sharing the treasured letter of congratulations that he received as a schoolboy, as well as to those who contributed their handwriting to help me create or re-create some model letters: Elliot Rothman, Alison Shepherd Lewis, Annie Zeybekoglu, Abby Miner, Sue Toigo, Eleanor Lewis, Peter Vanderwarker, and Margaret Fitzwilliam. Mari Oye and Colin McSwiggen kindly granted permission to use the letter on page 186, on behalf of the group of Presidential Scholars who signed it.

My sister, Alison, has been of particular help in tracking down family letters that we both remember but that only she had the sense to archive.

Peter Vanderwarker shot, and reshot, the author photograph on the book jacket.

I appreciate my author's "A team": my excellence-demanding editor, Rebecca Cole; her ever-alert assistant, Hallie Falquet; my far-seeing agent, Colleen Mohyde; and my superorganized coauthor, Sharon Cloud Hogan.

I also thank my long-suffering cousins, siblings, aunts, husband, and offspring. It takes a whole family to write a book.

Finally, I owe more than I can ever express to all the people in my life who should have gotten more letters back from me. This book is my way of saying thank you for all those decades of loyalty and patience.

INTRODUCTION

*Y*ou may think the personal letter has disappeared from modern life. Like many people, you may be ready to pronounce it dead, fearing that we have lost something precious. You might bemoan the pressures that seem to have plowed the warmth of the personal letter under in an avalanche of e-mail, cell-phone calls, greeting cards, and text messages.

The personal letter is not extinct, however—it's just evolving. Letter writing is very much alive: You can see this in the surging popularity of paper stores, in the near-sacred status of fine fountain pens, in the rubber stamps and glitter pens beloved of young writers, in the perennial appeal of traditional calligraphy, in the continued audience for popular books based on historical letters, in the ever-rising prices when celebrity letters are auctioned, and even in the hours that people still devote to typing to one another. E-mail and printout letters are new formats for some of the personal letters that used to be handwritten, and they make it easier to stay in touch in new ways.

Together, tradition and innovation are revitalizing the

art of the personal letter. Our yearning to connect has not gone away, nor have we outgrown most of the materials for writing or the occasions for letters. We can still write many warm, engaging letters in e-mail and printed-out pages as well as with pen and ink. It's all a matter of writing the best letters with the tools at hand.

If you are tempted to *write off* personal letters rather than *write* them, remind yourself of all the other good things people initially thought progress had wiped out of their lives. For the most important people and occasions, we put away the stainless steel and get out the family silver, turn off the fluorescent lights and light the candles. For a special treat, we skip the local movies and step out for a night of live theater. The most elegant modern weddings forgo the limo, carrying the bride and groom in an old-fashioned horse-drawn carriage. Our lives are a mix of both the cutting-edge and the time-honored arts, and our correspondence has followed this pattern. We still write letters, maybe even more than before—we just write them in a variety of forms. E-mail and printout letters have liberated us from having to handwrite everything we send, freeing us to write our most personal letters in whatever format makes the connection best.

Far from being marginalized, letter writing continues to be respected as a timeless art. Like other arts, it connects the artist with the viewer, and it leaves the viewer changed in some way. Artists in every new generation find new forms and materials to express common human experiences. As the Victorian essayist Walter Pater wrote, "Art comes to you proposing frankly to give nothing but the highest quality to your moments as they pass." A personal letter, well composed and sincerely meant, will add a dimension to your life that only art can provide.

The personal letter is still alive; there goes your excuse for not writing! The good news? With this book, you can learn to use letters to strengthen your most treasured relationships.

PART I

How to
Craft a
Personal Letter

Of all the arts in which the wise excel
Nature's chief masterpiece is writing well.

—John Sheffield

*A*s you start to acquaint—or reacquaint—yourself with the art of the personal letter, remember how easily you can make it a natural part of your everyday life. You already write, type, and send e-mail; you own most of the tools you need; you already have your own personal style; and you have a basic understanding of the parts of a letter. You just need to improve what you already know how to do and then put it to use more often, in order to keep you in better touch with the people who matter. As you read through the first part of this book, you'll pick up dozens of useful tips and reminders that will help you send a letter whenever you have something to say—even if it's nothing more than "I am thinking of you."

The first four chapters will help you consider all the forms your letters can take and how much better they can be. Then, once you've learned how to add artistry to what you write, the second part of this book will guide you in choosing the right words for life's occasions.

CHAPTER 1

The Art of Connecting

What a lot we lost when we stopped writing letters!
You can't reread a phone call.

—Liz Carpenter

You're so connected. You check your messages from a gizmo in your pocket, a laptop on your kitchen table, and a desktop in your office. You read e-mail from work while you are at home and personal e-mail on the job. You send out jokes, photos, breaking news, invitations, and announcements. You phone people between classes, on the train, and before a concert. (When you phone from the bus, you always seem to sit next to me!) You leave lots of messages, often timing your calls to avoid actually talking to anybody in person. You buzz your friends' cell phones with telegraphic short text messages, converse in real-time cyberspace with instant messages, and add a sticky note to any piece of paper you send around.

Although you've traded quality for quantity, you've still got all your connections covered. You don't even buy a quart of milk without a quick text message home to see who wants fat-free and who wants 1 percent. Your family and friends know that you're thinking of them, even when those thoughts only come out as "How r u?" on their cell-phone screens. You may not feel sure that you've used exactly the right format for every message, but overall, you're so connected, you couldn't be missing anything. Or could you?

In spite of all of your efforts, you may still be missing the most satisfying, expansive, resilient, creative way to keep in touch—the personal letter.

HOW IS A LETTER DIFFERENT FROM A NOTE?

A personal letter takes longer to write than the few abrupt sentences you bang out without proofreading before you click on "send"; it takes longer to read than the blink-and-delete blitz that helps you purge your in-box; and it digs deeper than the brief handwritten note that you drop in the mail. A letter deals with issues that deserve more than a minute of attention. It aims to strengthen a relationship, not just react to a situation. A letter isn't limited to a specific message like "Can you come over?" or "Thank you for the birthday check." Rather, it can take both the writer and reader on an excursion that sets off from a home base of mutual trust: "I know you'll be interested in what I think" or "I'd like to hear your ideas on this." Whether it comes into your life onscreen or through the mail slot, the well-thought-out personal letter is irresistible to read aloud, mull over, respond to, read again, and save.

Good letter writing feels much like good conversation, and it has the same power to nourish a relationship. It even includes the same critical ingredient of taking turns, since the best way to start writing a letter is to begin where the two of you left off, by picturing your last get-together or by rereading whatever the person sent to you. Letters allow your conversation—and your thoughts about each other—to amble along at a leisurely pace, even while other parts of your lives are galloping by.

The next time you need to connect with someone who matters, on a subject that requires more than a snap reply, stop and ask yourself, Is there a better way to do this? Is your connection as warm and strong as it could be? Think about what it feels like to settle into a personal letter that's been written just for you. Remember how connected it makes you feel, how valued and cared for. Couldn't you use more of that in your life? Whether it arrives in an envelope or on a computer screen, the personal letter is a small masterpiece in the art of staying connected.

Personal letters carry thoughts and feelings that don't come through as clearly any other way. They tap into a rich stream of history, send your reader unmistakable proof that you care, and offer an outlet for your creativity.

Even though you appreciate this lost art, you may still doubt your ability to be this kind of artist. Let's try to pinpoint what is holding you back. Is it the time involved? Are you at a loss for what to say or how to say it? Do you worry about the rules of letter writing? Although you will find in this book a wealth of guidance and ideas to get you started, remember that the aim of letter writing, like any art, is better expression and connection. The point is not to create perfect letters, but to reach out to the people you care about in a more engaging way.

WHAT YOU WILL FIND IN THIS BOOK

The first part of this book covers the basic tools and formats, as well as fresh ideas to help you feel confident about what and how you write. The second part includes tips for writing common kinds of letters, with sample letters to inspire you to write (or type) on your own. All you need to do is focus on how satisfying letter writing can be. Like walking to the store instead of driving, you can build your letter-writing muscle by finding ways to integrate letters into your routine. Just because you can send short messages the moment they enter your head doesn't mean you have to. Start now; each letter you write will make it easier to write the next one. If you're skeptical about how to fit letters into your crowded schedule, relax. You don't have to unplug your computer and go back to hand-cut quill pens on monogrammed paper. Instead, you can learn to take the best that the traditional letter has to offer and use it to add sparkle and civility to everything you write, type, print, attach, or e-mail. This book will show you how.

CHOOSE YOUR FORMAT

Your message, of course, forms the core of your letter, but before you choose your words, you'll need to decide on the best way to present them. Does the occasion call for ink on paper, or would a nicely worded e-mail be the best vehicle to convey your thoughts? Should you print out a typed letter and mail it in an envelope, or attach it to an e-mail? There is no one right choice. Most personal letters can take different forms to fit different situations and relationships. Before you begin, ask yourself how the format you choose will affect the way your message will be interpreted. Doing this will help you to make better choices, and to appreciate and interpret other people's choices when you read their letters.

Because people can't help noticing, on some level, how you choose to present your ideas, your choice of format becomes an integral part of the message. In addition to the literal meaning of your words, the visual qualities of your format provide clues to your reader about how to interpret your letter. Your timing and your choice of materials also convey messages about your relationship with your reader. Pencil on notebook paper says "I didn't forget your birthday" to your mother, but it says "I'm really clueless" to your boss's wife. A letter written by hand on Cartier stationery suggests a stronger effort to apologize to an offended hostess than a hasty e-mail message, even when it contains exactly the same words. On the other hand, a long, reassuring e-mail letter of support that comes half an hour after your best friend has called in a crisis will do much more good than the same words that arrive four days later on paper. A senator's office staff may, as a matter of policy, give more weight to a well-worded defense of your position, typed neatly on personal letterhead and signed, than they give to a checked-off, standardized postcard—in fact, they may even show your letter to the senator. And a letter to a long-lost high-school friend will call up a clearer mental picture of you if it arrives in your handwriting on good stationery than if it pops up in her e-mail in-box.

Today there are three major ways to send a personal letter; each of them has strengths and weaknesses:

- You can handwrite a letter and send it by mail.
- You can send a letter by e-mail.
- You can type a letter as a computer text document. Then, you can either print it out and mail it in an envelope or attach it to an e-mail.

There's no uniform rule for how to send which words, when, and to whom. As in all art, the ideal makes compromises with the real. You might prefer to write a long letter of advice to your daughter at college to accompany the check she suddenly needs you to send, but reality may dictate that you transfer the money to her account from your desktop computer and type your advice into an e-mail attachment that she'll open right away. In contrast, your occasional letter to your grandfather may give him much more pleasure if it arrives on paper with a family photograph or a news clipping enclosed for him to share with his friends than it would if it appeared in an e-mail in-box that he seldom opens.

Learn to trust your own instincts when you choose a format for your letter. Listen to the little voice that murmurs either "Maybe this one deserves more effort" or "Don't worry so much this time; just get it there somehow." There are many ways to improve your letter, no matter how you send it. Although one format may be more communicative than another, any letter is better than no letter at all. Don't let your aspiration to come up with the perfect missive get in the way of your effort to create one that is good enough.

When you feel comfortable with the format you choose, your authentic writing voice will stay in tune and resonate more clearly. You may give voice to a different part of yourself in what you scrawl on plain paper than in what you write in your careful calligraphy on keepsake-quality paper stock, but you're still expressing *you*. Just as the same two people will have a different conversation in a pizza parlor, a French restaurant, or at a church coffee hour, each form of a personal letter can bring out a different side of your relationship.

To make your letters most personal, you'll need to strike a balance between what comes easily for you and the extra effort that you can expend to make them the best they can be. Keeping this balance in mind, let's look at each format's strengths and weaknesses.

Handwritten Letters

Writing by hand sets the gold standard for making yourself truly present to your reader. Traditional pen-and-paper letters offer many unique advantages. Handwritten letters feel intensely personal, weaving together your ideas with the visual art of words, color, and texture. They offer unimpeachable evidence that you believe the reader, the message, and the relationship are worth your time and your undivided attention. Letters that you handwrite on paper not only look good; they smell good and feel good, too.

Writing by hand requires only a few widely available low-tech, low-cost materials and tools that you can use anywhere, without needing a computer, Internet access, special know-how, or a place to plug in. Physically durable, letters can be archived by the recipient and reread by anyone decades—even centuries—later without special technology. A stamp that costs a couple of quarters sends them anywhere in the country, and a dollar or two sends them around the world. People welcome a handwritten letter as an ambassador from a more civilized age, and they are ready to extend that extra courtesy to the words they read and the person who wrote them. And nowadays, sheer novelty means that the person who receives a handwritten letter in the mail will sit up and take special notice of it, and of you.

Handwritten letters do have their disadvantages, though. Their delivery can be maddeningly slow and unpredictable, ranging from overnight to a full week, with no mail deliveries or pickups on Sunday and holidays. If the address or postage is wrong, the envelope may not be returned to the sender for weeks. The reader who is accustomed to hitting the reply button may take longer—or forever—to make the effort to write back by hand. Also, handwritten text can be hard to revise and correct, writing by hand can be slower than typing, and handwritten letters may be hard to write or difficult to read. The act of handwriting itself, less a matter of routine today, makes some writers overly prim and self-conscious when they pick up a pen.

If you decide to handwrite a letter, don't let concerns about these potential pitfalls hold you back. You don't have to reach impossible standards of eloquence and beauty. If your intention is to connect with your reader in the most personal way possible, just the extra effort you put into ink on paper will be greeted with appreciation and delight.

Letters That Are Printed Out or Attached to E-mail

You can send the next best thing to a handwritten personal letter by typing your words into a document and printing them out to mail in an envelope. You can also send a typed letter immediately by attaching it to an e-mail. With some planning and good judgment, this format can offer the best of both worlds—the time and attention that go into a well-crafted letter, plus control over the timing of its delivery.

Printout letters are easy to draft, revise, save, and go back to later, and they benefit from the computer's spell-check system and grammar suggestions. If you print these letters and mail them, you can make them more personal by adding a few sentences in your own handwriting, or by making a creative statement through your choice of paper, font, point size, type color, spacing, and margins. A recipient with poor eyesight can download the document you have attached to an e-mail and enlarge the font size or zoom in closer for easy reading. In addition, you can keep a permanent copy of what you wrote on disc or in your "sent" file.

Like e-mail, however, printout letters require electricity, a computer, and a printer, and if they are sent through the post office, they will spend a few days in transit. Printout letters can turn a normally fluent writer into a nitpicking, typography-crazed perfectionist (like me!), more obsessed with margins, fonts, and dingbats than with actual thoughts and feelings. Or it can reduce the most fluent calligrapher to a two-fingered hunt-and-pecker. And despite all the care that the writer puts into typing, printing, and mailing, some readers may feel that printout letters are just too impersonal, almost commercial, as compared with handwritten ones.

Sometimes this hybrid medium feels just right, though, for both the writer and reader. Requiring only a little more time than you would spend on an e-mail message, a letter that comes from your keyboard can feel almost as personal as a letter that flows from your pen.

E-mail Letters

Unlike handwritten or printed-out mail, the words that you type on a computer and send over the Internet can arrive instantly, on any day, and at any hour. Once you have access to a computer and a Web connection, this kind of letter is virtually free. You can connect to the Internet for a small fee in cafés and airports, and at no charge in public libraries. Quite a few cities provide free access to everyone in their business districts. With e-mail, most messages with wrong addresses bounce back immediately, so that you can quickly correct an address, then send the message out again right away. You don't have to be at your home address to open your e-mail, or arrange for it to be held or forwarded when you travel; it follows you on business trips and vacations. You can read and answer your e-mails at your leisure and mail your replies off in a few seconds or minutes. High-speed connections let you send messages with graphics, decorative fonts, attachments, and other bells and whistles. Sometimes you can literally add bells and whistles! Both the writer and the reader can easily file and archive the e-mails they have sent and received, find them by date, search through them by word, and forward copies on to others. If the type is too small to be read easily, the reader or writer can simply make it bigger on the screen.

On the minus side, however, most e-mail looks stark, and it is limited to a one-size-fits-all layout that militates against readability or enjoyment. The screen setup is stiff, tight, sometimes surrounded by advertising, and hard to modify for artistic expression. Some people don't use e-mail at all, and some who have it don't check it regularly. And everyone knows someone who knows someone whose e-mail addresses and files disappeared one day on the server—poof—with no trace left behind.

Just as writing by hand on paper can raise the writer's standards for wording, typing into an e-mail frame can lower them. Many people abandon careful spelling, basic grammar, and common courtesy once they click on the button to compose a new message. The tone of a person's e-mail message may also sound out of character: e-mail makes some writers apologetic and verbose, whereas others come across as being blunt and offhand. It may be difficult for the writer to infuse the e-mail screen with the same warmth and personality that come naturally in a handwritten message on paper.

The reader's response to the e-mail format can also be unpredictable. Some readers may react negatively to it; older ones may still not be accustomed to using a keyboard to write a letter or be comfortable with reading one on a screen, whereas young ones may have discovered a newer and cooler way to stay in touch. They may write and read e-mail, but it doesn't necessarily make them feel connected. Some traditionalists, who prefer the civilized standards of a handwritten letter, view this modern letter format as one of today's barbarians at the gate.

E-mail is here to stay, and it suits many occasions almost as well as letters that are handwritten or printed out. Use it whenever it helps you stay in touch.

Regardless of format, the important thing is to write a letter, and write it better; throughout this book, you will find plenty of ways to make any letter format feel more personal.

CONSIDER YOUR READER

As you choose the format for your letter, strive to balance your own talents and limitations with your reader's needs and expectations. Your family and friends include people of different ages and abilities; meet them on their own terms whenever you can.

Some formats will be easier for your recipient to read and reply to than others. To ensure that your format works for and not against the two of you, take into account your reader's potential problems with reading, writing, hearing, and speaking. For instance, e-mail, rather than handwritten letters, can offer a lifeline to a person with Parkinson's disease, because his hand tremors make it difficult to hold a letter or write one by hand. A phone call, in contrast, will help you connect with a person who cannot use a keyboard or pen without pain because of multiple sclerosis. And most people who are sick or injured can manage to read, or be read to, from a sheet of paper.

Sometimes you may not be able to determine from afar exactly which format would be best. Once again, take care to think about the person who will receive your personal letter, but don't get so hung up on the right format for your message that you fail to communicate at all. You may just need to take more care with your words, no matter how you send them.

As you consider your reader's physical abilities, also consider his "attitude handicaps." Writing a personal letter brings you into the other person's world, complete with his peeves, prejudices, and paranoia. Your grandfather might be disappointed to receive an e-mail thank-you note when he expected a handwritten letter. Yet people may surprise you with their communication habits and their homegrown etiquette opinions. Your otherwise old-fashioned uncle may check his e-mail four times a day, whereas your teen-age daughter may lavish hours on one handwritten, glitter-encrusted, rubber-stamped masterpiece to send to her best friend. In letter writing, as in real life, you have to deal with the friends and family you've got.

If you don't know the best choice of format for your reader, stay alert for cues such as the following:

- What has he said to you about his preferences and aversions?
- How computer-savvy is he? Does he know how to open an attachment? Are your systems compatible for attachments? Is he connected by dial-up or broadband?
- Does he check his mailbox or e-mail regularly?
- How good is his eyesight, hearing, handwriting, and typewriting?
- Does he collect memorabilia or maintain scrapbooks as a hobby? Or does he tend to get rid of clutter by throwing letters away?

I've learned to work with the letter-reading oddities of my husband, an engineer who for decades has been "too busy" to open his paper mail. Now I sort it daily, save the handwritten gems to read aloud later, shove the bills under his keyboard, and e-mail any news to him that will require his immediate attention. Though we gossip, argue, and murmur out loud with each other just as much as we ever did, new formats have added more threads to the ties that bind us. We e-mail back and forth, on topics that range from a schedule change to a thank-you for taking out the trash to a long ramble on the meaning of life—even when I'm sitting fifteen feet away from his desk! When I mention an interesting item in the newspaper, he'll look it up online. When I ask his advice about what I'm writing, he prefers to edit an attachment rather than a printout on paper.

Whatever format you choose, your letters can strengthen the connection between you and each of the people who matter to you. The next chapter will show you how to give your letters a personal touch.

CHAPTER 2

The Tools of the Trade

I'll call for pen and ink, and write my mind.
—Shakespeare, Henry VI, Part 1

Just as your choice of letter format can convey a message of its very own, the devices that put ink on the page or pixels on the screen can influence the way the reader will imagine your voice. For that reason, you should write the words that matter with the best tools and materials you can possibly afford.

PEN AND INK FOR HANDWRITING

Pen

The biggest single improvement you can make to your handwriting—for ease of writing, reading, and enjoyment—is to write with a better pen. Although convenience puts a ballpoint pen into most people's hands, there are other choices that you should consider: roller-ball pens, markers, and fountain pens.

Invented in the 1930s, the ballpoint pen may be practical, cheap, reliable, and ubiquitous, but it sucks the life out of good handwriting. Even skilled calligraphers find it difficult to write a beautiful page with a ballpoint. Because you have to press down hard enough on the ballpoint tip to keep the ink flowing, it becomes more difficult to shape the natural curves of a legible script, and the resulting line itself is thin and visually monotonous. A ballpoint is the old bathrobe of pens, not really up to greeting a friend. (Still, it's better than pencil on lined notebook paper, the T-shirt and undershorts of the letter-writing wardrobe.)

HOW TO IMPROVE YOUR HANDWRITING WHEN YOU USE A BALLPOINT

- Put two sheets of paper under your stationery to pad a hard surface. The pen will flow better, skip less, and make a darker line. (Don't write on a squishy surface like a single sheet of paper on cloth or felt, or the padded surface of a mailing envelope, because the point of the pen will poke right through.)
- If the ballpoint clogs, flick the tip quickly through a flame and then wipe it before writing.
- Store your ballpoints retracted if possible, and pointing up.

Without doing anything else to make your handwriting more expressive, you can still ease your writing strain by trading up, either to a roller-ball pen, which is similar to a ballpoint pen but uses smoother-flowing ink, or to a marker pen, which swabs the ink onto the page through a tiny rigid fiber tip. The free flow of ink will relax your hand and mind. Without finger strain, your hand will move more smoothly, making more natural letter shapes.

Once you see how much easier it is to write with a roller-ball pen or marker, and how much better your script looks, you might be inspired to go one step further and explore the traditional look and feel of a fountain pen. The ink flows freely from the fountain pen's metal nib onto the page, making a clean, intense, dark line. In addition, a metal nib offers you a choice of "footprint" (the area where the nib touches the paper), so that your writing line widens and narrows a little with each change of direction. A standard nib that ends in a square stub improves your script right away by varying the line just enough to intrigue the eye.

The ultimate, most expressive, user-friendly writing instrument is a calligraphy fountain pen. Its chisel-shaped ink nib creates the dramatically contrasting thick and thin line of italic calligraphy, which is unmatched in artistry, readability, and appeal. The calligraphic line and the classic italic letter shape will add interest and grace to your handwriting. If you'd like more information on calligraphy history and lessons, you can read my book *Learn Calligraphy*.

TIPS ON BUYING AND KEEPING A PEN

- If you choose an expensive pen, check to make sure it is covered by a lifetime warranty and find out where you can get it repaired. Many companies that sell high-priced pens maintain service departments and respond to e-mail and telephone inquiries.
- If you know you are absentminded, don't carry your expensive pen everywhere with you. Instead, carry a cheap, good-enough pen in your pocket or your purse, so you won't be upset by every ding and scratch or devastated by its loss. Leave your best pen safely on your desk.
- Store your fountain pen pointing up, tightly capped. When you travel on an airplane, make sure the pen is full; changes in air pressure will push ink out only if there is a lot of air in the reservoir.
- Avoid pressing down hard on a calligraphy marker. You can

Choose the nib size and width that's best for your personal handwriting habits. If you write with a heavy hand, choose a blunt nib that won't dig into the paper or pick up fibers. If you write with large letters, don't use a thin nib. If you want to learn classic calligraphy with a chisel-tipped marker, practice at first with a wide nib to see your strokes clearly, but change to a narrow nib for handwriting your personal correspondence.

Buying a pen is like shopping for a car: Some people care passionately about the horsepower under the hood, whereas resharpen a frayed marker tip once or twice with a sharp blade by shaving the fuzzy fibers down to the hard core.

- If you're not sure whether a fountain pen will improve your writing, you can get the feel of its flow with an inexpensive Pilot Varsity disposable fountain pen for less than $10. This type of pen has its own 1.8-gram ink supply, which the manufacturer claims will write a third of a mile before running out.

- Purists don't lend their fountain pens. The pen might get lost, or the borrower's different writing angle can wear and twist the nib minutely, so that it feels strange after it's returned.

- Consider your own special needs when you choose a pen. If you are left-handed, for instance, a roller-ball model may not be your best choice, because the wet ink may smear too easily onto your hand.

others want to spend their money on leather seats and a burled-walnut dashboard. (There's even a Harley-Davidson pen from Waterman that capitalizes on the look and feel of luxury horsepower.) The best gold-iridium fountain-pen nib will top out around $200, and even the very best ballpoint pen refill still costs less than $5—most luxury ballpoint bodies are fitted with $2 refills. Be clear with yourself about what matters to you—engine power or curb appeal—so that the pen you buy feels good in your hand and writes well on the page. Any high-quality pen nib should glide over the paper and last for years, but the pen that simply looks beautiful in your pocket can improve your writing, too. A beautiful pen that you choose for its looks may inspire you to write for the sheer pleasure of holding and seeing the pen, whereas the same nib in a plain body just may not get your artistic juices flowing.

Ink

Traditional etiquette, early chemistry, and the pen's anatomy restricted letter writers a century ago to filling their fountain pens with blue, black, sepia, or blue-black ink from a bottle of ink on their desks. Today, you can pen your personal letter in every color from apple red to zucchini green if it looks right to you. You can choose from half a dozen colors of ballpoint ink and some two-dozen colors for roller-ball and marker pens. Fountain-pen ink cartridges are available in standard colors as well as red, sepia, purple, and green. You can also retrofit your cartridge pen with a permanent reservoir and fill it from a bottle of classic blue-black ink on your desk.

Manufacturers formulate the viscosity of their inks to match the internal tolerances of their fountain-pen nibs. Although your ink brand may be limited by your pen's requirements, you can usually choose between washable ink, which is paler and may smear, and permanent ink, which makes for sharp, indelible, smudge-free writing but which will also linger for days under your fingernails and will never wash out of your cuffs. I have had to decorate many of my favorite shirts and trousers with oddly placed embroidered flowers to cover up these inevitable ink spots.

Regardless of which type of ink you choose, the ink color should contrast enough with your paper color to be easy to read. No blue ink on blue paper, please, and save white ink on black paper for short, dramatic notes.

PRINTERS

Current printer technology for home use offers you two main choices: ink-jet printers and laser printers. If you don't mind paying a high price for the ink cartridges, then an ink-jet printer will let you and your readers enjoy the expressiveness of color printing. Its slightly slower printing speed won't matter for a personal letter that is a few pages long. Although laser printers are still mainly limited to black printing and cost more at first, they do produce sharp, high-quality letter images at much faster speeds and allow you to save money on ink toner in the long run.

PAPER

When you shop for paper, you face a wealth of choices. Although some papers are compatible with many different printers and pens, others have more restricted uses. Regardless of whether you shop in a store that specializes in office supplies, stationery, crafts, or art supplies, you should form some idea of what to look for and what to avoid.

Your writing or typing will look more personal on something other than stark white copy paper, yet a very unusual paper may complicate your task. When you're just starting out, choose a writable or printable paper, a smooth but not slick surface, an off-white color, and a minimum of background texture. Then, as you write more letters, you can broaden your search to consider more adventurous choices.

It's not enough to choose your paper on the basis of your first impression of its looks alone, since the right paper fiber and surface can also make your words easier to write and to read. The wrong paper for your pen can make letter writing an infuriating, disappointing chore; the wrong paper for your printer can jam or wrinkle, repel the ink, or blot it up. Think about the kind of pen or printer you plan to use. Take your printer's model number or your pen with you to the store. Ask the clerk about fibers, textures, colors, weights, edges, size, and imprints. The following pages will help you to understand your range of choices and show you how to use the language of paper to describe what you want.

Paper Fiber

Paper is made from a wide range of tiny fibers. When shopping for paper, match the paper fiber to your pen or printer. Paper manufacturers tailor many of their fibers and surfaces specifically for either pens or digital printers, whereas other papers work best for arts and crafts projects.

The cheapest paper, designed for magazines and news print, is made from wood that has been ground into dust; better paper is made from chips of wood that have been chemically broken down into a pulp of longer fibers. High-quality paper is made of a mixture of cotton or linen scraps and no more than 50 percent wood pulp. It sometimes includes recycled fibers. For unique visual interest, you can find specialty papers made of mulberry leaves, banana peels, worn-out blue jeans, or—I'm not making this up—elephant dung!

Paper fibers range from fine to rough. In addition, paper may have tiny visible bits, called "inclusions," that contrast with the main pulp fibers. Consider the visual interest added by large or small recycled fibers, bark, glitter, flower petals, or leaves. Inclusions may make writing and reading more complicated, but they add a depth to your printed or handwritten letter that words on a screen just can't match.

Paper Texture

Texture refers both to what your eyes can see and to what your fingers can feel. To make paper, a slurry of wet pulp is streamed onto a smooth wire screen, where the pulp then settles into an overall texture called "wove." Pulp can also be streamed onto a ridged wire grid that makes a lined pattern called "laid." Although a woven texture is more common, a laid finish can help you to keep your handwritten lines straight. When you hold laid paper up to the light or lay it over a dark background, you can see its grid texture more clearly.

The wire screen also may contain a raised insignia that shows through high-quality finished paper as a translucent watermark. Like laid texture, this feature can be seen most clearly by holding the paper up to the light. Truly devoted writers who crave the ultimate visual luxury can custom-order a carton of paper watermarked with their own personal insignia.

Newly made wet sheets of paper are squeezed through wringers to dry and smooth them; hot rollers make a smoother surface, a process called "hot press," and cold rollers leave a rougher surface, called "cold press." Most writing and printer papers are hot-pressed.

A thin coat of transparent gel, called "size" (also called "sizing," which helps distinguish it from the paper's width and height), smoothes many paper surfaces further and keeps them from sucking up ink like a paper towel. Most paper that is designated as stationery and sold expressly for hand-written correspondence is very thinly coated with sizing. Most copier and printer paper is hot-pressed and uncoated. Thick, shiny sizing that coats the surface of specialized photograph paper produces extremely sharp, accurate printed images, but it is too slippery for handwriting. Arts and crafts papers are usually pressed and sized specifically for certain inks, paints, or glues, rather than for pens or printers.

During manufacture, when damp paper is passed through rollers to smooth and dry it, one roller may be set to roll slightly faster, burnishing one side into more of a shine. Your paper package may have a "this way up" arrow, or you can hold the stack vertically to check for a slight convex curve. To tell if the front of your page has a different finish from its back, you can also test the way that it feels between your fingers and thumb. If your ballpoint pen slips, try the rougher side; if your printer ink or fountain-pen ink soaks in unevenly, try the smoother side. The ink used in Sharpie markers will penetrate most standard paper, staining the back and sometimes the next sheet.

To avoid surprises, don't buy any paper until you've handled it and folded it, and don't buy large quantities until you've printed or written on it and sent it through the mail.

TYPES OF PAPER

Personal stationery paper combines linen or cotton fibers (which are usually specified on the box or visible by holding a sheet up to the light to see the watermark), a hot-press surface, and a very thin layer of sizing. You can best write by hand on this paper; the surface of most stationery is not made for ink-jet printers, nor do standard sizes of personal stationery fit the regular 8½-by-11-inch business-size document format.

Printer paper or *bond paper* is made mostly of coarser, cheaper wood pulp, rather than finer, more expensive cotton and linen fiber; it may soak up some fountain-pen inks unevenly. It is not usually coated, but pressed very smooth between hot rollers. Although most uncoated printer paper does not enhance fountain-pen handwriting, because it drinks up too much ink or drags on the nib, sometimes through trial and error you can find sheets that will work with your pen.

Paper Color

Paper fiber itself comes in many different natural colors and can be bleached or dyed further in the factory's vat before it flows into sheets. The resulting half-dozen standard colors (such as goldenrod or pink) of inexpensive printer paper may feel too familiar to have much artistic value. Reasonably

Arts and crafts paper may jolt your pen with surface bumps or snag the point with loose fibers that drag an extra trail of ink along. Those enchanting, picturesque surface textures of watercolor, pastel, and scrapbook papers may disappoint you by shrugging off ink from your pen or gulping up ink from your printer. A roller-ball pen or marker may follow the ups and downs better, but ultimately, a ballpoint may be the only way you can bulldoze a written path through the underbrush to impose a readable line on some of these unusual paper surfaces.

Photo paper, which is coated with a thin layer of shiny white clay paint, permits printer ink to make a sharp image, but it doesn't help your handwriting. Your wet fountain-pen ink will dissolve this surface coating and then dry up into glue immediately, tugging repeatedly at the metal pen point if you slow down. Smudges of oil from the skin of your hand may prevent smooth ink coverage by laying down invisible waterproof patches on the paper. Even ballpoint inks may skip, slip, blob, or smear. Save shiny paper for photographs.

priced personal stationery, however, is available in dozens of appealing off-whites, such as gray, buff, and cream, as well as in soft blue, pale pink, and ecru.

In general, colors balance well with their opposites; for instance, cool midnight blue ink balances warm cream paper, whereas dark, warm red ink looks elegant on cool pale gray paper. Whether you choose your ink or paper color first, consider these classic, classy combinations: black ink on buff paper, sepia on white, and purple on cream. Then try combinations of your own.

Don't hesitate to express yourself through your choice of paper color. Color sets the tone, subtly giving the reader extra clues about who you are and what you want to say. In addition, paper and ink together can evoke the culture of the past like a historic costume. Fashions of the past can inspire your paper and ink palette. You may see yourself in the timeless buttoned-down simplicity of bluish black ink on white paper, the classic nineteenth-century period suit of dark sepia on pale "Lincoln blue" paper, the medieval echo of black and red on parchment paper, or the 1960s mod flamboyance of dark purple ink on bright orange, yellow, or lime green paper.

Paper color, however, requires the same caution you would use with perfume or background music: If it looks too vivid, it drowns out your words. If your reader's first reaction is "Orange and purple?" instead of "Fun!," maybe you'd be better off expressing some of your buoyant personality through your words instead. If you want an intense color or an ornate pattern, but you suspect that readers might be overwhelmed, then choosing envelopes that are lined with such paper will give them a whiff rather than a wallop.

COMBINATIONS OF PAPER AND INK

Pale paper colors:	Cream	Ecru	Sage	Blue	Gray
Strong ink colors:	*Blue or Purple*	*Blue-black*	*Blue or Sepia*	*Sepia*	*Red*
Strong paper colors:	Tan	Turquoise	Yellow	Green	
Complementary ink colors:	*Black*	*Sepia*	*Purple*	*Sepia*	

Try some of these ink colors with white stationery that has a contrasting one-eighth-inch band of color printed at its very edge.

Paper Weight

In addition to its fiber, texture, and color, look at the paper's thickness and feel its weight. Heft it in your hand and rub it between your fingers; hold it upright and see how easily it droops. Paper can be thick or thin, fluffy or dense. Think about whether you want to be able to write on both the back and front of the page without your ink showing through, consider how to fold it for the envelope, and picture the reader unfolding the sheet and holding it to read the words. Do you want it to curve softly in the hand or stand up stiff and straight?

When you tell the salesperson what you are looking for, it helps if you learn to speak the language of paper. For instance, "twenty-pound paper" means the weight of five hundred sheets (a ream) of full poster-size paper before it is cut down into pages for writing or printing. Standard printer paper is between eighteen and twenty-two pounds. For a sheet that looks and feels more elegant, try twenty-eight-pound paper and up.

If you expect to write long letters on just one side of the page, then thin sheets will fold more easily and cost less to mail. If you want to write on both sides of the sheet or send your letters in unlined envelopes, stay away from paper that is less than twenty-four pounds. Some paper is so thick that you can't fold it smoothly unless you score it (and then it can't be unfolded without cracking). This kind of paper is more suitable for unfolded note cards than for folded letters—or for sending, without folds, in a large flat envelope.

HOW TO FOLD YOUR LETTER

- Letters look most personal on stationery paper that is slightly smaller than printer paper, written as whole pages and then folded in thirds.
- If you need to fit a standard-size sheet of printer paper into a smaller, more personal envelope, fold it in half, then in half again or in thirds.
- For occasional dramatic, ceremonial, or archival letters, send them unfolded in a large flat envelope.

Paper Edges

You can choose the kind of paper edge you like—either a straight machine-cut edge or a soft, frayed-looking edge called "deckle." Deckle, which comes from the German word for *cover,* refers to the frame outside the wire screen used in making paper by hand. Even though the first thing traditional printers or stationers always did was to trim off the uneven quarter inch they regarded as a messy dust catcher, if you want to give your letter an antiquarian look, you can tear your own deckle-edge pages from larger sheets. Pull the pages against a sharp tabletop or ruler edge, fold them loosely and tear them with a blunt edge, or hand-cut them with a specially designed jagged paper cutter, punch, or scissors available from crafts stores and Web sites.

Paper Size

The human body, historical accident, social prejudice, machine requirements, and personal whim have all governed the dimensions of stationery. Before steam power mechanized the manufacture of paper around 1800, paper was produced in single handmade sheets on frames small enough for a strong man to hold in his outstretched arms and dip, one at a time, into a vat of wet pulp and lift out. These frames varied in size. To make book or writing paper, the manufacturer folded and then cut these whole sheets into smaller sheets, which were usually one-eighth, one-twelfth, or one-sixteenth of the original, but since the large sheets came in many different original dimensions, the sizes of the fractional sheets varied, too. To this day, the sizes of even "standard" printer paper are slightly different depending on where it originated—for example, 8½ × 11 inches in North America and 8 × 11½ inches in the United Kingdom.

Until postal-delivery regulations were revised in the mid-nineteenth century, the recipient, not the sender, paid for postage. Small paper, densely filled on both sides with tiny writing (which often also crisscrossed itself and covered the inside of the envelope), was generally accepted as being the size most considerate of the reader's budget. Before she earned her own money from her novels, Jane Austen fretted perpetually about how much the letters she received from her beloved sister, Cassandra, were costing her out of the allowance from one of their brothers.

Only two generations ago, people's choice of stationery size conveyed a clear message about their personality and gender, the subject matter, their social status, and their relationship to the reader. Stationers offered more than twenty-four distinct sizes of stationery, each with its own official name and each with its strictly specified use and user. In England, these social distinctions were as obvious to the eye as the difference between an Oxford accent and Cockney slang was to the ear. Well-bred gentlemen and ladies each wrote in the appropriate script style, which was

GUIDELINES FOR CHOOSING STATIONERY SIZE

- Standard 8½ x 11-inch copy or printer paper will give your letter the look of ordinary business, rather than personal connection. That impersonal feeling disappears if you trim it even one-half inch smaller.
- Letter-size stationery, from 8 x 10 inches down to about 5 x 7 inches, immediately identifies your letter as being warmer than a business letter and broader than a handwritten note, sending a strong signal that you will cover personal topics at leisure. An envelope smaller than the usual business-size envelope sets the tone, as well.
- Note cards or single-fold notepaper suggests that you will cover one topic briefly. Such notes necessarily follow the formal, almost formulaic structure and haiku-like word compression of a typical thank-you note.
- Letter stationery of exaggerated size or unusual proportions —square, elongated, or multifold—showcases vivid individuality and extra care on special occasions.

conspicuously different from the business hand of legions of clerical drudges. They used their own specific proper sizes of paper, sending a letter of introduction in manly script on Baronet paper or an invitation in a feminine hand on a dainty tea-length card. A bride acquired a stationery "wardrobe," along with her trousseau, for the social demands of first getting married and then being married; in the event of her husband's death, she switched to special paper with a wide black border prescribed for her first year of widowhood and a narrow border allowed thereafter. In an age of subtle social distinctions, sending words on the wrong piece of paper, like using the wrong fork, could be a major faux pas.

Today, paper comes in mercifully fewer sizes, and mistakes are less world-shaking and more forgivable. You can write notes on any cards or folded paper the size of a paperback book and letters on any sheet smaller than a magazine. Certain sizes, however, still send a strong signal about what your letter is going say. For example, standard white copy paper prepares the reader to talk business across a desk, whereas notepaper forecasts the kind of brief chat on one topic you would share standing up, and a letter on personal stationery sets the stage for the kind of comfortable conversation you might exchange while sitting down.

Paper Imprints

If a sheet of stationery seems too plain for your personal style, choose one with an imprint. Many stationery papers are sold with designs already printed on them, from a hairline frame or decorative border to a small symbol, leaf, or object to a small scene nestling in one corner or a big one lightly covering the whole page. You can also have your sta-

WHAT TO DO WHEN YOU CHOOSE PERSONALLY IMPRINTED STATIONERY

- If you don't know much about printing terms such as *engraving, thermography, photo offsetting,* and *embossing,* don't place a special order until you have seen and felt real samples. Look at how the printed sheet appears from the back, too, and when it is held up to the light.

- If you plan to run printed stationery through your laser printer, remember that the hot rollers that fuse the ink toner will melt any thermographically printed image.

- If you'll be moving soon, imprint only your name on the letter paper. You can add your new address later with newly printed envelopes or a printed sticker.

- Keep your letterhead or imprint relatively small, thereby allowing ample space for writing.

- If you plan to write by hand, don't choose an elaborate script for your name imprint—it will clash with your own writing.

- You might prefer to have only your address imprinted on stationery and envelopes, so that everyone in the household can use them.

- If you plan to write multiple-page letters, order unprinted matching sheets for the later pages.

- You may be able to use your letterhead design for ordering custom note cards, too, which will save you money on the make-ready charges.

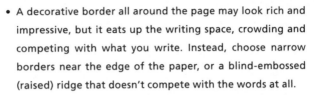

- A decorative border all around the page may look rich and impressive, but it eats up the writing space, crowding and competing with what you write. Instead, choose narrow borders near the edge of the paper, or a blind-embossed (raised) ridge that doesn't compete with the words at all.
- Look at all of the available color choices for printing ink, and consider blind embossing—raising but not inking the letters. This technique requires an extra charge for making the custom die, but it gives your monogram or letterhead a classy and understated look.

tionery custom-printed with your own initial, monogram, first name, last name, or address.

Don't let a prim obsession with the proper paper keep you from writing on whatever you can find when you have something to say. Paper is beautiful and inspiring, but it should serve, not enslave, your ideas. My daughter Lily, spending her first Thanksgiving away from home, captured some nostalgic insights to send to her family by writing in the margins of a new members' sign-up card as she sat in church. The future president John Kennedy, marooned in 1942 with his men on a South Pacific island, scratched his plea for rescue on the side of a coconut.

BEYOND WHAT THE READER SEES: DECORATIONS FOR YOUR DESK

Writing a personal letter is like home-cooking a meal—it's one of the everyday human pleasures that sometimes rises to the level of a sacred ritual, complete with special objects that add extra meaning. You probably cook with your own quirky assortment of familiar spoons and pans, and enjoy the color, furniture, and decoration you've created in your kitchen. Of course you could arrange it more logically, but then it wouldn't be you. And whether you cook from scratch or open a box, it's still the same kitchen you've organized to create the food you offer to the people you care about.

Inspirational Items

Your writing desk can hold the same kind of personal treasures as your kitchen, to reinforce the same human pleasure of creating something that connects you with friends and family. When you're elevating an everyday chore into a work of art, a few magic wands come in handy. My mother's simple onyx fountain-pen stand, which inspires me every day at my desk, still evokes my childhood awe of the power of the handwritten word to persuade a teacher to excuse a grade-school absence.

Whether you write longhand or tap on a keyboard, you

can treat yourself to whatever will help you best express
yourself. The ancient Chinese tradition of respect for calligraphy enshrined brush, ink stick, ink stone, and paper as
the "four treasures of the study," also giving reverence to
the optional pen stand, ink box, paperweight, seal, and seal
box. Whether you arrange them as curiosities, collectibles,
or conveniences, your own desk treasures might include
glass or marble paperweights, old-fashioned pen stands,
crystal inkstands, chamois pen wipers, stamp cases, decorative blotter corners, handheld blotters, Florentine marbled
folios, silver sand sifters, rulers, and penknives—whatever

THE CIRCULAR FILE

You probably have a box or folder near your desk where you can
carefully preserve any letter that marks a special occasion, that you
want to read again, or that helps you feel connected to the writer.
It is even more important, however, to buy yourself an especially
nice wastebasket. Learn to throw away any letter that sours your
connection, regardless of whether the poison comes from someone
else's pen or your own.

Whether you write letters by hand, print documents out, or
send e-mail, learn to "store as draft" by simply sleeping on any letter you think doesn't quite say what you mean. And then toss out
any incoming or outgoing mail that could possibly damage your relationships.

links you to your past and to the larger community of past and future letter writers.

Don't overlook the inspirational power of what you wear, listen to, sip from, and gaze at while you write. Jo March in Louisa May Alcott's *Little Women* signaled to her family, and herself, that "Genius burns" whenever she put on her ritual writing cap. Some people need absolute silence, a clean desk, strong coffee, and a view of a brick wall; other people tell me they write much better with some Vivaldi on their earphones, the smell of flowers, a view of the ocean, and herbal tea in a favorite mug. Indulge yourself; these accessories can nurture your creativity as much as the right paper and pen.

Your desk itself can lure you to sit down more often to write. Light it well, sit up to it comfortably, and adjust it to a comfortable height. Listen to your body. My older brother, in his seventies, writes at a stand-up desk, but my daughters, in their twenties, prefer to write cross-legged on the floor or sprawled across their beds. Keep your writing tools handy in a favorite basket or box, and organize your stationery in a folio. Your addresses deserve good organization and regular updates in a book or a computer file. You might enjoy adding decorative touches to your computer, keyboard, and printer, to humanize the everyday flow of e-mail and print-out letters. You can enhance the letter-writing ritual with your own nostalgia, order, and fun.

Conveniences

In addition to their inspirational uplift, many writing accessories help to make writing physically easier. Blotting paper, for instance, cushions your stationery and protects your desk against stains and gouges. A pen wiper keeps any pen nib (and your fingers) clean. A postal scale, whether it is a tiny Victorian clip and counterweight or the latest high-tech device, will help when you consult the USPS.com Web site to figure the correct postage in a minute rather than wait in line at the post office. The less you have to struggle with the details of getting the ink out of the pen, onto the page, and into your reader's hands, the more you can focus on the essential task of making your personal letter a pleasure to look at and read.

Now that you know the basics of choosing pen, ink, and paper, the next section will show you how to make the most of those materials for your handwritten or printed letter, and help you rescue your e-mail letter from the digital doldrums.

CHAPTER 3

How to Give Your Letters a Personal Look

> Take pains and pleasures in constantly copying the best things
> you can find done by the hand of great masters. . . . Then you
> will find, if nature has granted you any imagination at all, that
> you will eventually acquire a style individual to yourself, and
> it cannot help being good; because your hand and your mind,
> being always accustomed to gather flowers,
> will ill know how to pluck thorns.
>
> —Cennino d'Andrea Cennini (c. 1370–c. 1440)

*Y*ou probably don't think of yourself as a calligrapher, and yet you already practice this art whenever you put a word on paper or on a screen. Every time you make the spoken word visible, you bring it into the real world of materials, shapes, colors, and textures, where what your readers see can carry as much meaning as what they read. You cannot duck all responsibility for how your words look on the page. Even no choice is a choice—default settings still add up to a style, and vanilla flavor is still a flavor. Over the centuries, calligraphers and type designers, along with millions of ordinary writers, have shaped an alphabet of powerful legibility, simplicity, flexibility, and beauty for you to enjoy.

The word *calligraphy* comes from two Greek words meaning "beautiful" and "writing," respectively. The influential type designer, writer, and teacher Edward Johnston broadly redefined calligraphy for modern revival more than a century ago as a way to "make good letters and arrange them well." This definition continues to guide us, even today, when most words are printed out or viewed on a screen. Anyone who writes or types—not just the trained artist— can still follow calligraphy's guiding principles.

The computer's potential for calligraphic excellence is no accident; in fact, it was embedded, early on, in the digital revolution. Steve Jobs, inventor of the Apple computer and himself an amateur calligrapher, underscored his belief in the power of good visual design in his commencement address at Stanford University in 2005. He noted, "The connection [between calligraphy on the page and typography on the screen] was there from the start." Many of the most engaging digital typefaces have come from designers with backgrounds in traditional calligraphy and typography— building on the best of the past rather than competing with it. As a result, if you learn even a little about better writing, you can then go on to "make good letters and arrange them well" with a keyboard as well as a pen.

Whether you frame your words in nineteenth-century

pen and ink, twentieth-century computer printout, or twenty-first-century e-mail, your thoughts will shine through. Although more and more people are becoming what sociologists call "platform agnostic"—ready to absorb information no matter how it arrives—this doesn't mean that it no longer matters how that information looks to them. By learning principles, rather than memorizing rules, you can welcome and use these new writing tools. Visual standards don't change from format to format, and good page design can always transcend the tools you write with. The few minutes you devote to improving your critical eye will enrich whatever you handwrite or type and will help all your words to look better.

The effort of getting your words onto the page or screen should not distract you from composing your thoughts into vivid and coherent words. Regardless of whether you write or type, your reader should be able to read and understand the meaning of your words without extra effort. And a pleasing page should allow both of you to participate in the letter as a lively creative art; even the best words will connect better when they're arranged well.

LETTERS THAT ARE EASY TO WRITE

Don't begin by worrying about how your writing looks; first judge how it feels. If you're not physically comfortable, your discomfort will interfere with your word choice and you may avoid writing letters at all. Even if you do succeed in grinding out the words, your tension and frustration will show. If, after a few minutes, the muscles hurt in your neck, back, arm, or hand, you should change your pen or keyboard, or your posture. Or change from pen to keyboard, or from keyboard to pen. Changing your attitude also can help; don't try to force yourself to write if it ties your hand in knots or to type if you just wear out two fingers in slow motion. Limber up for a minute so you don't start out with stiff chicken scratches or have to ditch a dried-up pen two sentences later. Stretch every five to ten minutes. Treat your handwriting like your face: you should aim for it to be clean, relaxed, and smiling—not stiff, tense, and groggy. Keep in mind that you may not be the best judge of your own legibility. Even handwriting that you think is not very good is usually good *enough*. Simply cross out errors with a single stroke, not a scribble.

Don't let your own impossibly high expectations keep you from writing by hand. A study by the Pilot pen company a few years ago showed that most people judge their own handwriting much more harshly than they judge other people's. A lot of people don't like the way their voice sounds on a recording or how their face looks in most photographs, either, but they still answer the telephone and smile for the camera.

LETTERS THAT ARE EASY TO READ

While you make your letter easy for yourself to write, make it easy for the recipient to read. Calligraphic clarity involves not just the individual letter strokes of your handwriting but the design of the whole page, as well. As long ago as 1922, when proper handwriting was more strictly taught and more highly esteemed, Emily Post said, "No matter how badly formed each individual letter may be, if the writing is consistent throughout, the page as a whole looks fairly well." If you leave enough space for what you are going to say and write in straight and level lines, your handwriting will clarify your thoughts for your reader.

Legibility also matters when you type. You can choose your font style, letter size, line spacing, and margins with an eye to letting your reader grasp your words without effort.

LETTERS THAT ARE EASY TO ENJOY

The *beauty* of your letter matters just as much as the ease of writing and reading it. Squint at your handwritten page or hold it at arm's length and turn it upside down. You can turn your on-screen document into a "thumbnail sketch" by zooming out from it until it's too small to read. This will activate your right brain, which looks and sees, and shush your left brain, which talks and reads. Quite apart from the meaning of the words, do you like everything else about your letter—its textures, colors, and proportions? Unless your readers are expert graphic designers or calligraphers, they won't analyze your choices one by one, but will respond to your letter in its organic entirety without knowing why. Until the invention of digital type fonts, many people didn't even notice the difference between typefaces, and even nowadays most people still don't realize they can change the standard default settings on their computers. If you have decided to use a favorite font and size for everything you type, your friends will think, "Oh, how nice, there's a letter from Joanne," rather than "Aha! If it's in Centaur fourteen-point bold double-spaced and compressed, with 1.1-inch margins, it must be Joanne using her special setting."

Most people instinctively recognize and respond to the faces of their friends and relatives, although few of them can explain why. Likewise, your loved ones probably won't be able to describe anything about your handwriting except that it belongs to you. They're not going to profile you as a serial murderer if you use what graphologists call "harpoons" to start some letters below the guidelines or happen to write two different forms of capital *I* on the same page. They'll simply look forward to what your letter holds. Even if the recipient of your letter knows you really well, all that he may be able to sense is how you are feeling in general by the overall tightness or looseness of your script, or a certain indefinable slant of your vertical letters.

If you don't quite trust your own artistic taste for color, margins, and letters, you can educate your eye by paying attention to how other people write. Decide what you like or dislike about particular writing styles and materials. Look again at the handwritten notes and letters you receive, not to judge them as good or bad but to break down what specific things make them easy to read and enjoy, analyzing the writers' artistic choices or ingrained habits that accentuate who they are. If you aren't receiving many handwritten letters, you can still observe people's handwriting or typing style during class, at work, in autograph catalogs, at flea markets, and in books. Whenever you're signing a guest book or passing around a group birthday card, study how people write their signatures. You can borrow specific elements from these small works of art to set a style for your own letters.

TECHNIQUES FOR BETTER HANDWRITING

Materials account for only half of the artistry of a personal letter. Good handwriting techniques can help you get the most out of the pen and paper you've chosen so carefully.

With a good technique, your gorgeous new Mont Blanc fountain pen won't drip and splutter, and even the letter you write with a modest black ballpoint on standard white printer paper can rise above the mundane. You'll be able to transform the chicken scratches you feel you're stuck with into a script you can't wait to share.

It's common practice to deplore the state of handwriting

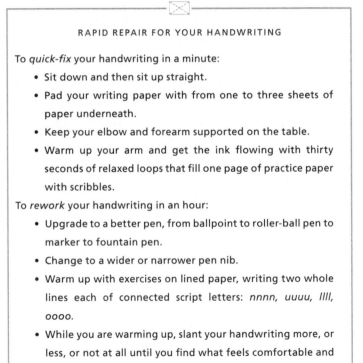

RAPID REPAIR FOR YOUR HANDWRITING

To *quick-fix* your handwriting in a minute:

- Sit down and then sit up straight.
- Pad your writing paper with from one to three sheets of paper underneath.
- Keep your elbow and forearm supported on the table.
- Warm up your arm and get the ink flowing with thirty seconds of relaxed loops that fill one page of practice paper with scribbles.

To *rework* your handwriting in an hour:

- Upgrade to a better pen, from ballpoint to roller-ball pen to marker to fountain pen.
- Change to a wider or narrower pen nib.
- Warm up with exercises on lined paper, writing two whole lines each of connected script letters: *nnnn, uuuu, llll, oooo.*
- While you are warming up, slant your handwriting more, or less, or not at all until you find what feels comfortable and looks readable and appealing.

today. Handwriting instruction in mid-twentieth-century America emerged from the straitjacket of the complicated, traditional Palmer method into the freedom—and chaos— of a variety of systems. Some regions and schools upgraded their programs to traditional italic, while others, under pressure to find more time to teach typing skills, tried various shortcut cursive systems. Still others abandoned ship,

- Isolate and practice any problem letters and letter combinations that you find hard to write or read (for instance, an *o* can slump into an *a* or open up into a *u*).
- Try to keep your lines of writing straight and level, the same distance apart, and contained inside at least one-half-inch margins.

To *restyle* your handwriting in a week or more:

- Go back to the roots of the alphabet. You can study and practice the chapter on classic italic in my book *Learn Calligraphy,* or sign up for a local short course or one-day workshop in calligraphy. Of course, you will not immediately master a classic italic cursive, which is the study of a lifetime, but your hand-and-eye coordination will improve. The letter shapes and their rhythmic pattern will slowly seep into your own script. You will also pick up the knack of visualizing and controlling how the whole page will look.

November 4, '09

Dear Caroline,

Cleaning the attic out for Mom was a real trip. Those tie-dyed bellbottoms we found got me thinking about how bizarre we looked. What were we thinking!?

I loved watching the twins, in their hip huggers and nose rings, giggle over snapshots of us. I have to take a lot of photos of them and save some of _their_ coolest outfits to get even.

I should also ask you about that box of Xmas tree ornaments. How are we going to divide those up with Kerry? Give me your ideas when we get that cup of tea two weeks from now in the Museum Café.

I can't wait. Thanks again for helping.

Love and corn candy,
Molly

From: Molly
To: Caroline
Subject: Sorting Was a Hoot
Date: May 12, 2008

Dear Caroline,

Cleaning the attic out for Mom was a real trip. Those tie-dyed bell-bottoms we found got me thinking about how bizarre we looked. What were we thinking!?

I loved watching the twins, in their hip-huggers and nose rings, giggle over snapshots of us. I have to take a lot of photos of them and save some of <u>their</u> coolest outfits to get even.

I should also ask you about that box of Xmas tree ornaments. How are we going to divide those up with Kerry? Give me your ideas when we get that cup of tea two weeks from now in the Museum Café.

I can't wait. Thanks again for helping.

Love and corn candy (oof),
Molly

This handwritten letter exemplifies the warm connection that paper and ink can make. The flowery stationery and pretty script add a smile to the words.

Though it sacrifices the visual immediacy and tactile connection of a paper letter for convenience, this e-mail version of the preceding handwritten and the following printout letters is warmed by typography.

letting children just speed up the capital letters they had learned in first grade and connect them as they wished. Regardless of what system you learned, you can build on your own method to develop a more useful and beautiful hand.

I have always believed that people are not stuck with their handwriting as it first comes out of the pen, just as they are not stuck with their face when they get up in the morning. You can improve whatever you've got. I flunked penmanship in third grade; if I could redesign my undistinguished script, so can you.

If you are not satisfied with how your words look, ask yourself how much improvement you want, and what kind. Then decide how much time you want to spend. You probably hover between those whose handwriting has just gotten a little rusty through neglect and those who know with deadly, daily certainty, that they were taught all wrong from the start.

At the same time, however, don't overcriticize what is distinctive about your script in your quest to improve it. If writing with a backward slant is a family habit, or if you learned to use all capitals in your training as an architect, or if you can't connect your letters to save your life, keep that basic style. Just build on what you can't change to make a letter from you a pleasure, not a puzzle, to read.

TECHNIQUES FOR BETTER PRINTOUT
AND E-MAIL PAGES

Unlike handwriting, word processing lets you easily correct your errors and rearrange what you've written. This process allows you to keep the best of both worlds: You can type and revise the document, print it, and then add handwritten notations on the paper copy to add breadth to your ideas and resonance to your visual voice before you mail it.

If you like to type but it hurts your muscles, reposition either your equipment or yourself. Just raising or lowering your chair can prevent a lot of pain and strain. Something as simple as lowering your desk surface or tipping your keyboard can make a big difference. Separate your screen display from your keyboard if you can. Your shoulders will be more comfortable if your hands type down near your lap, while your neck will feel better if your face looks straight ahead. Your forearms and your chin should be parallel to the ground. You may also benefit from expert advice in choosing an ergonomic chair and other equipment.

Finally, staring at a brightly lit screen in a pitch-dark room can give you eyestrain. Some ambient room lighting will ease the constant transition of looking from a dark keyboard to a lighted screen.

Coordinate your page margins with your type size. Aim for fewer than forty characters or from eight to ten words per line. Graphic design that you've put thought into adds your personal fingerprints all over your page.

Be careful not to overdo the typographic emphasis, though. DO NOT use all capitals for more than three words at a time, once per page. Don't "flame" people with a page of capital letters that raise your visual voice to a shout; capitals demand more effort to read as text than lowercase letters do. Use underlining, italics, contrasting fonts, color, highlighting, quotes, and boldface sparingly, only once per page, because each time you try to add emphasis, you dilute the overall impact of what is already there. Too much fiddling with the typography will slow you down and create a jerky, breathless, and melodramatic rhythm to your letters that can make them a chore to read. Let good word choice speak for itself by choosing type that doesn't distract attention. Keep in mind that some readers don't enjoy these novelties; the emoticons that make your sixth-grader smile :) may baffle his grandfather :-?

Your printout paper should harmonize with your choice of font. Don't overwhelm small, delicate type with a busy texture, or overdramatize big black letters on a featureless sheet of stark white copy paper.

Better Document Design

Whatever your keyboard skills, typographic changes can make your document or e-mail more readable. Try a font other than the computer's default setting, slightly modify its size and color, and put some thought into the spacing and margins so that your page has a signature style that subliminally looks like your "handwriting" to the reader. After you've experimented and printed out a trial page, make your choices and stick to them for personal letters. Reset your computer's default settings so that your chosen style is ready to use every time you type a letter. My favorite fonts happen to be Book Antiqua, Comic Sans, and Century Gothic. But "the beauty of letters, like that of faces, is as people opine," as eighteenth-century printer Thomas James said, and each person has different likes for different visual reasons. Thousands of font choices are available online in addition to the hundred or so that your software probably provides. The only limit on your font choice is the occasional difficulty that your reader's computer may have in displaying an unusual font that originates in your computer and arrives as an e-mail attachment; if the host computer can't display your font, it will supply a near match from its own selection of fonts.

Computer technology lets you vary your voice on paper and on screen. This voice seems to get louder with larger or bolder type, slows down with expanded spacing, and changes tone with a different font.

Dear Caroline,   November 4, 09

Cleaning the attic out for Mom was a real trip. Those tie-dyed
bell-bottoms we found got me thinking about how bizarre we
looked. What were we thinking!?

I loved watching the twins, in their hip-huggers and nose rings,
giggle over snapshots of us. I have to take a lot of photos of
them and save some of <u>their</u> coolest outfits to get even. ☺

I should also ask you about that box of Xmas tree ornaments.
How are we going to divide those up with Kerry? Give me your
ideas when we get that cup of tea two weeks from now in the
Museum Café.

I can't wait. Thanks again for helping.

Love and corn candy (oof),

Molly

---

*Using the same words as the letter on page 54, this document, printed
out on stationery, carries an echo of fun-filled nostalgia with its 14-
point font choice and simple layout. Typographic ornaments (emoticons)
add humor without overwhelming the text.*

Better E-mail Design

While e-mail stampedes into the technological future, it leaves its readers stuck in the artistic Stone Age. Visually primitive, it crams identically formatted messages into identical in-boxes, giving the writer very little control over how the words look on the "page." The format itself gets words in front of the reader simply and immediately, but it drains away virtually everything else that makes a personal letter so alive—the pleasure of anticipation, the visual expressiveness, the uniqueness of handwriting style and paper choice, and the evidence that the writer has put effort into the letter.

Even this bleakly mechanical format, however, can be animated with life.

Sending Attachments The simplest shortcut around the barren graphic landscape of e-mail is to retreat into the comfort of a typed document. Long e-mails are tiring to read. Scrolling through a long e-mail letter in the compressed e-mail frame won't satisfy your reader as much as settling down to read the same words properly arranged on a whole page. One solution is to greet your reader with "I'm going to attach my letter to you," then attach the document you have typed (or the image you have scanned in). Your reader can then open it and read it on the screen or print it out.

A few tips about attaching:

- Get to know who can open your attachments easily and who can't (depending on the limits of the person's system or skills). Ask the reader to let you know immediately if an attachment can't be opened, so you can paste the text into an e-mail or print it out and mail it.

- Try to keep the size of your attachments under 500 KB.

E-MAIL IS A BLUNT INSTRUMENT—SOFTEN IT

- Include your telephone and mailing address in the automatic signature, giving as much detail as you feel comfortable with. If you have a Web site, you can put the URL in the signature, too.

- Proofread. Turn on your spell-check system and pay attention to its suggestions. Misspelled words are like spinach between your teeth or crumbs in your mustache— they distract attention from what you say and announce that you're too busy to clean up your act. If something is worth writing, it's worth spelling right.

- Triple-check your subject box. A sloppily typed subject line will look like spam, alarming and possibly offending your reader. If they don't immediately recognize the sender's address, many people will mistake a badly titled e-mail for spam and delete it without opening it. Sometimes they will mark it as spam, thereby blocking future e-mails from you.

- Use your best, most complete words. Don't give in to the

- Whenever you type the word *attach* in an e-mail, go *immediately* to the file and attach it. Otherwise, you may end up forgetting and have to follow up with an "oops" e-mail, which the reader will open first. Everyone forgets; more than a century ago, even a genius like Lewis Carroll advised letter writers to go fetch any enclosure the minute they mentioned

---

temptation to dumb down what you say. Don't misuse the jargon of instant messaging or text messaging for your e-mails. Abbreviations such as *U, 4,* and *2,* which legitimately save thumbing in extra letters in the words *you, for,* and *to* on a cell-phone keypad, are unnecessary in e-mail that you send from a full-size keyboard. Don't make yourself look clueless, as well as lazy, just to save a few microseconds of typing.

- Refresh the subject box for some replies. When you send your brother your thoughts on your shared past, honor the occasion (and make it easier for him to retrieve your message from his archive) by giving your message a specific title, such as "What a good memory of Oakland Street your visit brought back!" instead of leaving the featureless cryptic "[none]" or piling up the even emptier "Re: Re: Re: Re: Re: [none]." In fact, you can upgrade your e-mail simply by hitting the compose key rather than the reply key, and giving a fresh title in the subject box whenever your reply will change the topic.

it. In *Eight or Nine Wise Words About Letter-Writing,* he wrote, "When you say, in your letter, 'I enclose [a] cheque for £5,' or 'I enclose John's letter for you to see,' leave off writing for a moment—go and get the document referred to—and *put it into the envelope.* Otherwise, you are pretty certain to find it lying about, *after the Post has gone."*

- When you reply to someone who has sent you an attached document or photograph, delete the attachment from your reply. You can set up some e-mail programs to do this automatically.
- Remember that, unlike your printout document, which includes whatever you see on your screen, whether you've saved your recent changes yet or not, your e-mail attaches only the version that you have actually saved.

E-mail Typography If you want to type your letter directly ito the e-mail frame, many systems will allow you to make simple changes to the font, color, and size of your letters, and very limited changes to the line length. Use these variations either all the way through to evoke personality or very occasionally to add emphasis.

Let in visual breathing space by hitting the return key an additional time between paragraphs. Break down a long block of text to separate a stream of ideas into a clear, organized list of bullets or numbers. You also can occasionally hand-justify the line length in lieu of using the standard margins. This is especially worth doing for short messages that are from fifteen to thirty words long—to create a small block of several lines of text rather than one long spindly string.

Before your e-mail design gets too ambitious for its format, remember that almost any change to standard e-mail will take more bits of memory, filling up your reader's inbox faster. Save bits! Don't hog bandwidth! And because

---

ABOUT COPIES AND BLIND COPIES

E-mail makes it easy to cc your personal letter to more people than the primary reader. You can spread the same good news to several people, let a third friend know what two of you have planned, or share a family memory with siblings. It's out in the open, frank, friendly, and fair; everyone can see who else is reading the letter.

It's all too tempting, then, to use the bcc button, which sends that blind copy to a third person without letting the first reader know. Why not?

If you've ever found out after (or during) a phone conversation that the person who called you had more people in the room listening in on the speakerphone, you know how an e-mail bcc can make everyone feel. Or maybe you were one of those people, eavesdropping on an unsuspecting friend with the listener's approval. Neither role leaves anybody feeling like a true friend.

The use of the bcc button is only appropriate at work, to avoid spreading one recipient's e-mail address around to everyone else.

some of your readers may still be connected to the Internet by slow dial-up, rather than by high-speed broadband, any seriously nonstandard e-mail graphics you send may take f-o-r-e-v-e-r to unfold on their screens.

If you want to refine your e-mail further, expert graphic designer Lance Hidy recommends using a twelve-point or larger font and enlarging the type for especially important details such as dates, times, and core messages. "Punctuation marks can be difficult to read on a screen, so try using two hyphens for a pause, with a space before and after— rather than a comma or a colon. The exclamation point ! is extremely hard to see, so put a space before it, and maybe make it bold if it is important ! Or use two !! Scan your handwritten signature, save it as a low-resolution file, and put it at the end of your e-mail letters." He also advises e-mail writers to stick with typefaces that every computer offers, preferably legible monoweight sans serifs designed specifically for digital display, such as Verdana. Otherwise, you don't know what your lovingly chosen font will look like when it arrives—it may have changed back from a typographic princess into a plain Cinderella.

BEYOND PAPER AND SCREEN

The art of the personal letter doesn't stop with ink on paper or dots on a screen. You can express yourself further with

enclosures and add-ons. Stamps, seals, and envelopes—
even the folds in the paper—all help build the frame that
showcases your thoughts.

Some letters on paper are like people getting ready to
step out—they're not fully dressed without a few accessories. Once you've written the words you want to say, you
can enhance how they look by your choice of envelopes,
stamps, enclosures, textures, and aromas.

Envelopes and Stamps

An envelope gift-wraps your letter and tells the reader that
this will be something special. It adds the luxury of visual
delight, shows that you took extra trouble, prolongs the sus-
pense, and sometimes even gives clues to the contents.

The envelope paper and color should match or harmonize with your stationery paper; envelope-lining paper adds
a subtle flash of color and design. The right envelope should
fit your one- or two-fold letter gracefully with up to one-
quarter-inch extra room. An envelope that is large enough
to deliver your page without any folds gives it a ceremonial
fanfare. For dramatic delivery of very large pieces of paper,
use a mailing tube.

You can print your return address, handwrite it, rubber-
stamp it, or stick it on with a label. Although the post office
prefers to see your return address on the upper-left front
corner, you can put it on the back if you wish. Use decora-

tive rubber stamps and stickers if they add meaning, putting them on the back of the envelope so they don't confuse automated address-reading machines. You can also write special instructions like "Do not open until your birthday."

Dress up your envelope with decorative stamps. My own favorite stamps happen to be those with the gold Arabic calligraphy that periodically honors the Islamic EID holiday (the festival that marks the end of Ramadan fasting), any stamp printed in turquoise and blue, and any commemoratives that honor my own home state of Iowa. You can even pay extra to have your own design or photograph printed onto a postage stamp, a service offered on the United States Postal Service Web site (USPS.com) and elsewhere.

Enclosures

You can give extra depth to your letter with an enclosure. A newspaper article about a mutual friend, for instance, is much more vivid than your secondhand report. A photograph makes you and your activities more real to the reader. Enclosures also can include small items such as a cartoon, a recipe, a lock of hair, or a sprig of lavender. Just remember that if the envelope is more than one-quarter inch thick, you must add extra postage and write "hand cancel" on the front of the envelope to prevent machine damage or nondelivery. If you send your neatnik girlfriend a pinch of sand from a

Cape Cod dune or confetti from your party, write a warning on the envelope so that she can guard against a mess on her floor. Make sure small single items are taped to a stiff card so they don't slip out of the envelope and escape.

SENSORY ACCESSORIES

- **Smell:** Some paper gives off its own natural or added scent. Ink, too, can carry its own aroma or a drop of your perfume. Use moderation!
- **Seal:** Melted sealing wax, stamped with a symbol or an initial, adds an antique embellishment. It has a hard time surviving modern post-office sorting machines without chipping off, however, and is best used inside, on the letter, and then mailed in an envelope marked "hand cancel."
- **Sound:** Sound can sometimes be added to e-mail. But watch it. You don't know who might be nearby to overhear. Put a warning in the subject box.
- **Touch:** Pay attention to how the paper feels. Your reader's fingertips will "read" this dimension of your letter subconsciously. What you print on the paper may add texture, too. My father, born in Victorian England, used to tell me about butlers who would surreptitiously rub a visiting card to feel if the new acquaintance was rich enough to have paid for costly raised engraving rather than cheap flat printing.

CHAPTER 4

The Essential Ingredients of a Personal Letter

Everything is proper as long as it's congenial.
—Julie Harris

W hether you write longhand or use digital technology, and whether your message is short or sprawling, cozy or ceremonial—all personal letters share a common structure. Each element in any work of art balances and harmonizes with the others. And like the best art, the best letters contain no unnecessary parts.

The main elements of your letter should resemble a real-life encounter, from greeting and exchanging pleasantries, through the heart of the discussion, to winding down and saying farewell. Because many letters also live on as documents that may be reread later by the recipient and discovered by others, you should locate your letter in a specific time and place with a date and return address.

Although most of a letter's structure is logical and self-explanatory, even the few rules that may seem arbitrary still deserve to be followed, because they show your desire to connect by meeting your reader's expectations.

THE DATE

The date traditionally occupies the upper right-hand part of the first page of a letter. Of course, if you are sending your letter by e-mail, the date is automatically included, along with the precise time of day.

If you're writing by hand or printing your letter out, don't just jot "Wednesday" or "February 6" at the top of your page. Provide the full date, month, and year. The more you use words instead of numerals, the more traditional, leisurely, clear, and personal your letter will be. Consider the difference in clarity between "02–06–09" and "February 6, 2009." Europeans and some military personnel customarily write the date in a different order, "6 February 2009," and sometimes shorten it to "6 II 09," writing the month as a Roman numeral to prevent confusion. Others use the high-tech sequence of year/month/day: 09/02/06. In the United States, however, it's most common to see the following form: Feb. 6, 2009.

THE SALUTATION

You wouldn't encounter a friend and just start talking without saying hello and addressing the person by name, and you wouldn't start a telephone call by launching right into your main message. Likewise, you should always begin your letter with a salutation.

You won't offend anyone if you use the salutation "Dear," which accommodates a parent, spouse, classmate, roommate, coworker, newspaper editor, neighbor, or friend.

If the standard "Dear Fred," just doesn't seem warm enough for your relationship, you can escalate to "My dear Fred" or "Dearest Fred." For a cozier, more affectionate tone, you can try "Fred, dear" or a pet nickname such as "Fredster."

Titles belong in the salutation of a personal letter if they underscore family relationships, as in "Dear Grandpa Fred," "Dear Grandpa Fiske," or "Dear Grandpa," or when you know that the person prefers it, as in "Dear Mr. Formal." If you would like to be on closer terms with someone, start your letter "Dear Fred Formal" but sign at the end with your first name only. Continue to greet him as "Mr. Formal" until he has signed his own reply to you with "Fred."

When you write a personal letter in an e-mail, don't omit the salutation that introduces any message longer than one sentence. "Dear Fred" is still universally appropriate. Size up how modern your reader is: "Hello, Fred," or "Good morning, Fred," or simply "Fred," will set a tone of informality that may strike Fred as either refreshing or irritating. "Hey," "Dude," or "Yo" serves as a civilized salutation only at a certain age and in certain circles; you know who you are.

THE BODY OF THE LETTER

You'll write a better letter if you have a sense of what you want to cover before you start. Follow the classic advice for the most effective speeches: Tell them what you're going to tell them, tell them, and then tell them what you just told them.

The Beginning

In a handwritten letter, set the scene with specific small talk, such as "How is the new job going?" or "I can't wait to try the new shortbread recipe that you sent," rather than overly familiar clichés, such as "How are you? I am fine. Long time no see." Omit routine weather reports and other transient topics such as "I have a headache" or "Dave is so upset about his sleepless night"; these trivial matters will be even more trivial by the time the letter arrives at its destination.

Map out the particular purpose of your letter. If you are going to ask the reader to reply or take other action, such as,

"I'm writing to share with you some of the plans for Katy's wedding so that you can let me know soon about making reservations," mention that in your opening paragraph.

The less frequently you write back and forth to each other, the more polite padding you'll need at the beginning. A lively correspondence can jump right back into the ongoing stream with "What a great idea" or "You could help with that project."

At the start of an e-mail letter, introduce your main topic, briefly and specifically, in the subject box. Unlike a mailed letter, your e-mail can include small talk about the weather, current headlines, and how you feel, since this news will still be fresh when it arrives.

The Middle

Write about subjects that concern you both. You can share news about your own thoughts and projects, as well as make genuine inquiries about the other person's ideas and activities. If you intend to mention several related ideas in this part of your letter (for example, to praise specific achievements in a letter of congratulations or to include special memories in a letter of condolence), jot down a short list before you begin to write so you'll be sure to cover everything.

If your letter is going to include criticism, sugarcoat it with praise or gratitude in order to keep the reader reading and sweeten the pill.

As you start winding down, prepare for an exit with some conventional courtesies. Repetition of your sympathy, concern, or thanks should be expressed here, rather than in the closing. A sentence that starts "Again . . ." or "Let me repeat . . ." allows you to reaffirm your opening idea.

The Closing

Printed or handwritten personal letters will sound both friendly and courteous when you close with "Love," "Yours," "Fondly," "Warmly," "With love," "Love to all," "As ever," or "As always."

Your choice of a closing should mirror the loving hug, warm kiss, polite handshake, or casual wave that you would use to wind up a conversation in person.

Many two-word closings can feel impersonal and businesslike: "Yours sincerely," "Truly yours," "Yours truly," or "Sincerely yours."

The casual tone of e-mail has given rise to the use of neutral or casual good-byes, such as "Best regards," "Cheers," "Best wishes," "Ciao," and "TTFN" ("ta-ta for now"). Although conventional handwritten closings translate comfortably into e-mail, e-mail closings may feel too offhand in a handwritten or printed letter. A few closings work in any format: "Best regards," "Regards," "Sincerely," or "All the best."

THE SIGNATURE

A personal letter almost always ends with your first name as a signature. Sign both your first and last name only if your letter covers a serious issue that you want to add weight to, or when it commemorates an important occasion, or when it aims to begin an acquaintance with someone you know only slightly. Sign your single initial to give a breezy, intimate tone to a letter. Sign your nickname if your reader expects it and if you prefer it.

Although preferences vary among families, some parents of grown children may enjoy the new egalitarian relationship that comes with the use of first names.

THE POSTSCRIPT

If rereading what you have handwritten or printed out makes you wonder whether you have made yourself clear, you can add a comment in the margin, insert it with a caret($^$), or footnote it with an asterisk (*). If you have completely left an important point out of your letter, add it in a brief postscript. Confine yourself to one P.S. only! A second P.S. makes your thoughts seem fragmented, and a third means you should write a second letter after you have gathered your wits.

Rambling and proliferating postscripts, some of them

longer than the letter they follow, have annoyed readers for a long time. Even Francis Bacon, generally intent on more important issues, took the time to complain about a sixteenth-century correspondent: "When he wrote a letter, he would put that which was most material in the postscript, as if it had been a by-matter."

If you have sealed up the envelope before your ideas all took shape, remember that any P.S. you write on the outside of the envelope will be read first, perhaps mystifying the reader without its context. Similarly, if you need to add a postscript to an already-sent e-mail, keep in mind that the reader may open it before opening the longer letter itself and so it may not make sense. Title any such postscript clearly in the subject box to indicate that it should be read after the main letter.

THE ENVELOPE OR E-MAIL HEADING

The more complete the address on the envelope, the more likely it is that the letter will be delivered quickly. For instance, adding the apartment or condominium number to a building's street address can cut one day off delivery time. Rural delivery (RD) addresses require careful attention to route numbers and road names, and their sequence. Always include a zip code, checking with the U.S. Postal Service Web site (USPS.com) for accuracy. Give the zip code a whole line to itself. Most European addresses include an essential four- or five-digit number unique to the household, just before the city name.

Always write, print, sticker, or rubber-stamp your return address on the envelope. For privacy, you may wish to use just your address and not your name. Include at least your last name if you think the reader may not identify you from your address on the outside of the envelope, your handwriting, and your first name on the letter inside. The post office prefers the placement of the return address in the envelope's upper left front corner. You can also write it vertically along the short end of the envelope or centered on the back flap. If your stationery page is not imprinted with your address, you can also include it above the date on the letter page or after your signature. Since many people throw away the envelope, the easier it is to find your address inside, the more likely your reader will be to write back.

In e-mail, your reader's address and your return address (as well as the date and time) appear automatically, identifying you immediately and making replies immune to error. A cryptic e-mail address such as "djnomadic246" or any unfamiliar e-mail address, however, may mystify people who don't hear from you often by e-mail, and they may delete your letter as spam. If your reader might not recognize who you are from your e-mail address, give her a clue in the subject box, with a title such as "A long-delayed letter from Carolyn" or "Childhood memories of Edmund," and sign with your first and last names, not just your initial or nickname.

Your e-mail address, unlike a return address on an envelope, offers no clue to where you are in the real world unless you mention it in what you write, or set your e-mail signature option to contain your other contact information. There's no reason not to include this extra courtesy when you write personal letters by e-mail, especially if you hope someday to receive replies in the postal mail.

Shaped by logic and humanized by custom, the personal letter has evolved over the centuries into an elegantly designed device to convey thoughts. Classic letter structure adapts itself to virtually any writer, any message, and any reader. You can build on this armature, confident that your letter will be read with clarity and trust. In the rest of this book, illustrations of the kinds of personal letters that you are most likely to write demonstrate the creative potential that structure can give to your ideas.

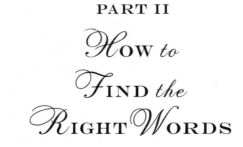

PART II

How to
Find the
Right Words

*People hunger for more attention. . . . Full attention will
be the aphrodisiac of the future.*

—Linda Stone, a former software techie, as quoted by
columnist Ellen Goodman in "A Snail Mail Tale,"
Boston Globe, August 14, 2005

*O*nce you've begun to discover or rediscover the personal letter, you'll find many reasons to write one, whether you want to raise a toast or offer to eat crow. You may already be taking advantage of opportunities to connect by picking up the phone, sending a greeting card, meeting for coffee, hashing it out over dinner, or cheering from the bleachers. You don't have to change what you are doing, but you can build on it. Thoughtful, well-written letters can take your friendships and family ties beyond the level that your conversations, phone calls, and brief notes have already reached.

The many kinds of letters in the chapters that follow offer simple, specific ways to elevate your words into a small work of creative art. They range from the focused intimacy of a grandparent's legacy letter to a newborn to the semipersonal formality of a citizen's heartfelt letter of conscience to the president. These examples, all of them actual letters or closely based on real letters, show how vital this form of communication can be in everyday life. They embody ideas from this book's previous chapters, which explained how to make choices, not just follow rules. They show what the art of the personal letter can achieve, offering you the kind of insight that you used to find every day in your mailbox.

Each kind of letter brings together format, materials, techniques, and wording to create a clear sense of who wrote it, when, *why, and to whom—this sense of presence is so vivid that the letter still has the power to speak to us on its own, beyond the specific people and occasion that prompted it. Whether you are searching for suggestions for specific wording, or you want to guard against gaffes and omissions, or you just want to remind yourself how magical a letter can be, these letters will give you many hours of satisfying exploration.*

CHAPTER 5

Letters to Strengthen a Connection

*The great art of writing
is the art of making people real to themselves with words.*
—Logan Pearsall Smith, Afterthoughts, 1931

Somewhere between the great letters you *should* write and the daily messages you actually *do* write, you can spend a few minutes on the good letters you *could* write. A letter adds one more strand to whatever cord already connects you to others. It lets you develop a conversation that's slow, deep, and strong. You'll feel closer to people far away and stay up-to-date with those you see only now and then.

Even someone you live with may benefit more by reading your thoughts when you've collected and connected them than by hearing them whenever they pop into your head. You may find that writing by hand lets you focus on issues that you don't ever cover in daily phoning, e-mail, and face-to-face conversation, and frame them better. The sustained thoughts and complete sentences of a personal letter provide a nice change of pace from the furious staccato of daily or hourly e-mail conversation. It's like dressing up and going out to dinner together instead of snacking on warmed-up bits of this and that in your T-shirts at home—you're bound to talk about different subjects, with a different, probably better, choice of words. Just as you say more during a one-hour conversation than you ever in a dozen five-minute chats, you say more in a two-page letter than you ever would in twenty tiny notes about single subjects.

Try framing your words in a personal letter when you need to say "I'm thinking of you," "We miss you," "I've been thinking about what you said," or "Although I see you every day, I'm not sure that you know . . ." Why limit yourself to saying "Congratulations! Good job!" or "You were right and I was wrong" to your teenager when you can write it, too? If you spend extra time and effort to write it longhand or print it out, then leave it on her pillow, you might reach her on that channel when all the others seem jammed.

If you like the idea of the casual "just because" letter, don't wait for someone else to add this dimension to your relationship. Set an informal goal, such as writing a letter once a month to someone you'd like to be in better touch with. I write a lot of personal letters by hand—to atone for past neglect, or reactivate old friendships, or to stay on an older relative's wavelength, or just to feel better connected. You can trust that your letter, however you write it and word it, will be saved and reread.

RULES OF THUMB FOR WRITING A "STAYING CONNECTED" LETTER

Give your letter a core idea, no matter how slight. When a small daily event in your life makes you think of someone who would find it interesting, write a short letter to describe it. A funny phrase, a rediscovered photograph, a shared weakness for a certain kind of food, a relative's quirk, an old in joke, or a memento can jump-start a letter. Something minor in your world may still mean a lot in his.

As you write, don't be self-conscious, as though you were unused to presenting your thoughts with care. Relax. You're entitled to explore this art and make it your own.

Finally, keep trying. You may not receive the replies you dream of, but you can rest assured your letters connect you in extra ways with a person you care about. Even the best artists often aren't appreciated until people get used to their approach.

MAKE IT PERSONAL

Send your letter in the format you'd like to receive (whether it's an e-mail, a handwritten page, or a letter that you have printed out from your computer), but be happy with whatever form of letter he chooses to write in return.

Also, upgrade from your usual format whenever you want to show that you are putting in extra thought. If you send an e-mail to your brother every few days, an occasional letter on paper will show that you are putting more thought into some aspect of that daily stream of chat.

Add artistry, too—much as you tie a bow on a gift—with good stationery, a clear e-mail layout, or an appealing envelope. If you visualize your stay-in-touch letter as an exchange of small talk over a mug of coffee, the extra touches you add are like serving the cookies on a plate rather than straight out of the package. Even your e-mail will feel warmer and more conversational if you choose a friendlier type font.

CHOOSING THE RIGHT WORDS

- Paint a word picture with small specifics rather than vague generalities. "I thought of you when a little boy caught a pop fly at the game last night" brings the reader into your life more vividly than "We've sure had a lot of good times together." In *Writing Gooder,* Rhys Alexander wrote, "Detail makes the difference between boring and terrific writing. It's the difference between a pencil sketch and a lush oil painting. As a writer, words are your paint. Use all the colors."

- To get started, try one of these phrases:
    "I was just thinking . . ."
    "Something you said reminded me of . . ."
    "I've noticed something that might interest you."
    "I forgot to tell you . . ."
    "It's a beautiful day here. I thought you'd like to hear about what happened in our orchard last night."
- Instead of the trite "How are you? I am fine," ask questions that show genuine interest, such as "Are you back on your feet?" or "I'm halfway through unpacking."
- Be direct. Say, for example, "I wanted to ask how Janet's recovery is going" rather than just beat around the bush by asking, "How are things?"
- You don't really need the filler phrases "for your information," "if you'll excuse my mentioning it," "no offense, but," or "by the way." They make you sound reluctant to write what's on your mind.

A father writes to his grown-up daughter, using the art of the letter to elevate his thoughts into an heirloom to be treasured. No other format could have showcased these words as warmly.

Dear Amy,

Not enough paper to write down
all I think about you.

Not enough space to paint the colors
that come to mind when Amy talks.

Not enough notes for the music, both
sad and glad, that comes to mind.

Not enough ways to say I miss you.

Not enough fathers to say they need
their daughters

Not enough poetry to tell the sky
what you are to me.

Love, Dad

- *I* is good. *You* is better. *We* is best. Use all three. Consider the difference between "I want to be sure you were aware of all the compliments about Juanita's party. We saw the Ryans yesterday and they were raving about it" and just "Great party!"

Words spoken out loud often cannot deliver the emotional intensity of those written by hand. Don't miss the opportunity to write a letter in whatever format works for you, whenever your thoughts might bring you closer—whether the person you write to lives a thousand miles away or right next door.

CHAPTER 6

Letters to Home

*The one good thing about not seeing you
is that I can write you letters.*

—Svetlana Alliluyeva, Twenty Letters to a Friend, 1967

When you're away from home, sharing your journey in letters can comfort and inform the people at home who miss you, and writing them can help you feel better about the separation. A personal letter is a way to be less away. Your attitude and perspective opens a window onto what you experience while away from home, and writing to others about your world allows you to see it more clearly yourself. Someday, perhaps, your letters may become valuable documents that evoke a world and a time that has grown dim. If written with care, a letter home preserves the things that will still be important when time moves on.

It's well worth the effort to write a "real letter" to the people you miss. In making your world immediate for them, you may make it come alive someday for people you don't even know. For inspiration, look carefully at the letters that people used to write when written communication was the only link between home and away. You'll find them in biographies, museum collections, and maybe your own attic. Letters from soldiers, especially, are treasured and reread by their readers and senders both, and they are frequently kept for future generations.

Sometimes the thought of waiting several days for post-office delivery is enough to make you reach for your phone instead of your keyboard or pen. You might assume that if you get home before the mail arrives, the letter will somehow seem redundant. I used to think that a letter counted only if it got home before I did, until I noticed that some of the most interesting aspects of my trips got swept aside by the excitement of homecoming. You write things on paper that you don't always get around to saying, or don't say as well, when you are face-to-face again.

RULES OF THUMB FOR
WRITING A LETTER HOME

Begin your letter by greeting the reader with warmth, locate yourself in a specific place, and include the complete date.

Next, mention news about places and people you have

encountered, and send greetings to others as well as to the reader.

Don't complain, dwell on the transitory, raise problems without suggesting solutions, harp on things that can't be fixed (like the realities of the separation itself), or even mention the kind of problems that are going to be solved before the letter arrives (such as lost sleep, minor aches, and moods).

Likewise, don't mope or drop verbal bombs. Frame any difficulties in possible solutions. There's no need to repeat over and over how much you miss the people at home; this will undermine an adult's morale, drag down a teenager's normal steps toward independence, make a parent feel guilty, and upset a child. As Shakespeare wrote in *Macbeth,* "Things without all remedy should be without regard."

Give the reader specific details about your impressions of the places you've visited, the people you've met, and the ways in which these new experiences have transformed your way of thinking.

Last, reaffirm how connected you feel with the reader.

MAKE IT PERSONAL

Although personal e-mails can see you through the short rupture of a five-day business trip, longer separations call for you to get out your pen and paper. Your familiar handwriting, the actual paper that you touched, the stamps you've chosen, the moments of anticipation while opening the envelope, and the promise of extra items inside—all this makes you emotionally present to your reader with an intensity that e-mail just can't equal. A handwritten letter strongly evokes a sense of place, a world to visit anytime the reader rereads the letter. Even a printout letter can have this effect if you sign it, add a note, tuck in a souvenir, handwrite the address, and stick on a decorative local stamp. If a postcard is the best thing you have to write on, make it personal by filling it out like a note card and then mailing it in an envelope.

Choose paper that evokes your surroundings—a card with an image of a local scene, special stamps, stationery with a hotel letterhead, or a restaurant place mat. A college friend still smiles about a battered cardboard Cinzano drink coaster that her son sent her from Italy with a message scrawled across it. A text message from his cell phone wouldn't have had the same cachet, nor would it have turned up years later to make her smile.

Don't obsess over the proper stationery. Sometimes whatever you have handy to write on will display your words best. A close friend of mine treasures the only letter that her son in the U.S. Marines sent her from the war zone in Iraq. He tore off the lid of a cardboard box of Mexican rice mix, and in a four-by-six-inch space he wrote five hundred eloquent words and the complete address. Because mail from the front doesn't require a stamp, the upper corner held a single evocative word, "FREE." She told me, "It's amazing it arrived in the mail. He put everything he wanted to say in that one missive."

Use a printout letter when you have a lot to write about and you may want to send the same paragraphs of description to several people; then personalize the rest for each individual. Use e-mail when instant delivery matters most or when a letter would be hard to mail or receive a response to.

Finally, write your letter—in any format—even if you're not sure when you will be able to mail it. You'll feel more connected just by writing.

CHOOSING THE RIGHT WORDS

- Make associations between your world and the world of your reader. For instance, "I took a picture for you of a pub called Kiernan's Alehouse when I was in Ireland last week. The same spelling as your son's name!"
- Expand the connection by mentioning others: "Tell Mom that the scarf she sent has kept me warm all over Minnesota."
- Reflect on the effect that your journey has had on your worldview: "I never really appreciated how

Ocean View Cottages

48935 Shorefront Drive, Moravia Beach, SC, 29455

www.Oceanshoreproperties.com   800-345-6789

March 8, 01

Dear Maisie,

I'm comfortably settled here after a bumpy flight all the way. I was hoping for a few hours of rustic peace and quiet before the talk tomorrow. Remember how pretty it was when we were here 5 years ago? But as you can see from my addition to the letterhead, today it's mostly concrete & traffic. Technically, about 5% of the view still <u>does</u> have the ocean in it; I guess "Office View Cottages" just wouldn't have the same appeal...

I hope you can start that redecorating project while I'm out of your way; I'm not sure I told you what a good idea it is. And if you want to wait ~~and~~ for me to help, just do the creative part now and I'll pitch in with the heavy lifting. Just don't ask me what color!

I miss you a lot and hope Louisa is happy. Stay well; more soon.

Love and a hug,

Erik

frustrating the language must have been for Yu Yan
when she first moved to Texas until I visited that
village outside of Qufu, where not a single soul
spoke English."

- Underscore the strength of your relationship when
  you conclude your letter. As one nineteenth-century
  traveler wrote home, "If I were with you, I could
  talk enough to tire you."

---

*An academic on a short trip combines humor, information, small news,
and affection, to supplement the phoning and e-mailing that already
keep him connected in other ways.*

CHAPTER 7

Letters to Someone Who Is Away

To send a letter is a good way to go somewhere without moving anything but your heart.

—Essayist and teacher Phyllis Theroux

A personal letter can connect you to a child sleeping away at camp for the first time, a soldier facing stress and danger in the field, or a freshman immersed in a new identity at college. If they can't be with you, send a glimpse of your world in an envelope. What you write, and how you write it, can widen the frame beyond a picture of current events to evoke the larger landscape of home.

RULES OF THUMB FOR WRITING TO SOMEONE WHO IS AWAY

You write from a place where everything is familiar. Share that stability with a reader who is encountering new experiences all the time. Offer familiar handwriting, paper, expressions, in jokes, and topics. Update him on small local events, and mention news about mutual friends and relatives.

If you have a major change to relate or bad news to send, find a way to soften the blow. Use an intermediary such as a base chaplain, a camp director, or a college dean to help you get in touch by telephone or in person as soon as possible. Don't send alarming hints in the meantime.

Continue larger ongoing conversations, but don't assume that your reader is thinking exactly the same way that he was the last time you were in touch. Don't make too many assumptions about what your reader is going through. In addition, ask about long-term plans and ideas.

Stay positive. Keep alive the image of home as a place to come back to eventually and not somewhere that is unraveling during his absence. If a raccoon sampled the Thanksgiving pies cooling on the back porch while Mom was taking a nap, spin it into a good story, not a disaster. Present larger problems in terms of your ability to handle them, and lower the urgency of your trivial troubles.

As you close your letter, reiterate your basic faith in the reasons that force the separation—such as support for a soldier's mission or approval of a child's adventure. End on a high note.

Wed, Aug 7, 91

Dear Penny,

By now you'll be comfortable in Cabin Seven at Camp Wapsi Y, learning all about life in the woods. I was so glad to see where you'll be living and to meet the girls who bunk with you. They looked friendly and fun. They all seemed to have ten-ton duffel bags, too.

Dad sends his love & says he'll mail you a postcard from his fishing trip. They plan not to get lost (but they said that last year.) He could use that map-reading course I saw in your camp catalog.

I bet you'll have lots of good stories to tell. More soon.

Big hug,
Mom

MAKE IT PERSONAL

If you write in the same format and at predictable intervals, you can anchor your reader's images of home even while he is in a situation where other things may be unsettling. Writing by hand with pen on paper creates the most vivid sense of home, especially for people who know your handwriting well. Choose materials that somehow look like home—for instance, a card with an image of a local scene, or special stamps. If you own personally imprinted stationery, use it.

Add enclosures such as local newspaper clippings and photos to your letters from home to provide fun and information. Think twice, however, before you send news clippings to people living in countries with heated political situations and insecure postal delivery.

Let other people at home who might not manage to write a whole letter of their own add a few words to your page or an enclosure to your envelope.

Sometimes you'll want to type your letter on your computer, when you have phrasing you want to work on, or when you need to plan a long letter or need to keep a copy. A copy on file may be useful if a mailed letter goes astray or arrives late, or if you want to recall something you said before.

A letter to a ten-year-old camper strikes a brisk and upbeat tone, and keeps the focus on the camper, not on what she might be missing out on at home. The off-kilter signature of the page adds a whimsical note.

CHOOSING THE RIGHT WORDS

- Greet the reader with warmth. This is not a time to breeze past the "Dear . . ." salutation.
- Reaffirm the intensity of your connection with positive phrases. "We're proud of what you're doing," "I loved hearing your voice on the phone," or "I think of you every day" are much better than "I'm lonely," "It's so boring here without you," or "I miss you."

THINGS TO KEEP IN MIND WHEN WRITING TO A PERSON IN THE MILITARY

Soldiers have to spend months at a time away from home, often living in constant discomfort and random danger. Your letters should wish for him to stay safe, keep his morale up, and help him feel connected to the outside world—especially the world back home.

Don't write about politics. Focusing on the task at hand may leave a soldier no time or emotional energy to worry about global issues. Don't criticize policy or the president, who is a soldier's commander in chief.

Remember the realities of your soldier's surroundings: One young marine asked his mother not to send "pretty envelopes" to him when he was in boot camp because "the drill sergeant will punish me and the other guys will give me grief."

- Include some of your shared ritual punch lines and jokes, no matter how awkward they may look on paper. If you always use a funny nickname, use it in your letter. I started using "Mom Wow" one year when upside-down typography intrigued me, and now my daughters wonder what's wrong if I don't sign my letters and e-mails that way.
- Include other people when you say good-bye: "Mom joins me in sending you her love," "With love from all of us," or "With love from both of us to both of you."

THINGS TO KEEP IN MIND WHEN WRITING TO A COLLEGE STUDENT

When you write to any college student, leave out clingy, mushy sentiments. Your desire to write tenderly about how much you miss your little boy may far exceed your young man's desire to read it. Don't helicopter above his campus with your needy, fussy control. Avoid criticism, trivia, complaints, descriptions of conflicts at home, the preachiness of any sentence that starts "When I was your age," and clueless advice about what he should be doing at school.

Do include words of approval, encouragement, interesting news, funny anecdotes from home, and messages from others. Remember that what you write is not as important as keeping the channels of communication open.

THINGS TO KEEP IN MIND WHEN WRITING
TO A CHILD AT CAMP

Children often get homesick when they first arrive at camp, but by the time camp is over, they don't want to leave. Your letters can help by reassuring him that his home still exists while he is temporarily away, and by affirming his own newly established world.

Mail your first letter before he leaves, to ensure that it will be waiting for him when that first pang of homesickness strikes. Tuck a short letter into the footlocker of a first-time camper and maybe hand one to his counselor to deliver if the child needs a boost.

Your letters should not remind the child of how homesick he could feel. Blaze a trail for him toward autonomy with warm, light, upbeat bundles of news and encouragement, rather than heavy, emotional outpourings of attachment and worry. Set a good example by learning the camp rules, and don't regress by trying to sneak contraband cell-phone text messages to your child. Don't undermine the camp's agenda by focusing his attention on you and your needs. Write with open-ended questions, and keep the focus on the child's adventures at camp, not on what he is missing at home.

CHAPTER 8

"Keep Me on Your Radar" Letters

Good friends are hard to find, harder to leave,
and impossible to forget.

—Anonymous

Keeping in touch today may have left you, like many people, with a bulging in-box, calendar, voice-mail queue, and friend list, but a depleted emotional life. If you miss someone you used to feel close to, a personal letter may be the nicest way to reconnect.

In addition to reviving relationships that you've let lapse through neglect, you may wish to reestablish contact after something came between you. You may be the black sheep of the family looking to reenter the fold, a former resident who misses an acquaintance from the old neighborhood, or just someone who wants to refuel a friendship that ran out of gas. Don't let awkwardness keep you from making the effort to reconnect. Most people are flattered to be rediscovered by an old friend and will not hold the intervening months or years of silence against you.

RULES OF THUMB FOR WRITING A "KEEP ME ON YOUR RADAR" LETTER

At the beginning of your letter, reintroduce yourself and remind your reader about who you are, and were. Mention the nature of your old connection.

Next, describe where you are now, both in your life's journey and on the physical map. Also, inquire about the other person's life at present.

Express a wish for a continued or renewed connection. If you have an ulterior motive, it's usually best to be frank right away. I learned over the years that one of my acquaintances only wrote me to "get back in touch" when she needed a convenient place to stay on business trips; my recollection of feeling used has kept me from making the same mistake with my own old acquaintances, whom I keep in contact with solely for friendship.

Just as you would in an actual conversation, don't spill too much information right off the bat. Don't be too explicit. If you view this person as a confidante but she can barely recall who you are, your instant intimacy may put her off.

In closing, convey good wishes, and provide clear contact information for a reply. If you've proposed reconnecting once and received a neutral or frankly negative response, admit to yourself that the other person may just not be interested in resuming your relationship.

MAKE IT PERSONAL

Handwriting on stationery paper is a good cure for neglect. If you've let time slip by, show that you are making up for it now by taking time to write by hand. If it's been months or years, you don't need to save another three days by firing off an instant e-mail, except to inquire about an up-to-date mailing address.

What your reader sees and touches will remind her of you, so choose ink and paper that expresses who you are. Dress your words with the same care you'd use in selecting what to wear to meet someone after you've been apart. Without turning your letter into an art project or a formal document, show that you value the relationship and the other person's time.

CHOOSING THE RIGHT WORDS

- Use sentences like "I would like to get back in touch," "Let's catch up," or "It's been a long time."
- Leave until later the statement "I miss you." Instead,

Dear Robin,

I know you've heard by now that Hannah and I are getting a divorce. It's been a sad and painful process for us both, where nobody has come out ahead but still we feel relieved and ready to start fresh.

One extra loss for me is that you and Bruno won't, technically, be my relatives any longer. You've been a really good part of my life, and a source of a lot of support, and I hope we won't fall out of touch. H. has been a good sport about this "joint custody of the cousins," so you won't be choosing between us. To me, you're still family.

When I get resettled in a few months, I hope you'll be open to a letter or phone call now and then. And I would love to get together with you both next spring when I have a conference near San Diego. Again, thanks for ten good years of talk and companionship. I look forward to seeing you some day very soon.

Yours,
Rick

Temporary address: 33 Pennsylvania Avenue, Denver, CO 80234

E-mail may be your best bulwark against the unintentional rift that can occur when someone misplaces your address. It may be the best way to embed yourself in her mental and electronic files for the day when you can reconnect.

"I miss our friendship" or "I miss seeing you" may be more appropriate. The other person may have changed, or the situation may have changed.

- Don't leave the next steps vague with offers like "We must get together sometime." Offer a specific proposal that is easy to say yes to, such as, "Are you free for a cup of coffee at the Student Union any Tuesday in March?" Then offer an escape hatch that permits a graceful no, such as, "If this is not convenient for you, let's stay in touch and try again in May." Don't put the person on the spot with forced choices.

- Never ask for an apology after a long silence. Be the first to offer one, if you think one is called for at all (it usually is not). If you think your apology would help thaw the ice, read chapter 22 on how to say "I'm sorry" in a personal letter.

CHAPTER 9

Annual Holiday Letters

*Your letters are as good as a visit from somebody nice.
I love people who can write reams and reams
about themselves: it seems generous.*

—D. H. Lawrence, *from the* Selected Letters of D. H. Lawrence, *1997*

Sometimes you want to send the same words to a group in a letter that is personal but written for everyone. Although big events like a new baby or a wedding call for an announcement right away, for many people the passing of one year is reason enough to send out an update. The most familiar annual letter bursts into bloom every year for the December holidays.

The format, materials, and wording of your letter will give a clear signal to your readers, of course, that other people are receiving the same kind of letter from you. They won't know, nor will they care, exactly who else is on the list. Although the size of your distribution list can range from two dozen to two hundred, a variety of personal touches can keep this type of "broadcast letter" from becoming an impersonal newsletter.

Even with personal touches, though, individual tastes and local holiday customs can vary in ways that challenge the writer and leave a reader confused, amused, or dismayed. Customs differ from region to region and culture to culture. In Japan, for example, people choose their end-of-year cards from a narrow range of traditionally prescribed messages, and deliver them to the post office weeks ahead of time. The cards must arrive precisely on January 1, not later or earlier, to avoid a serious breach of etiquette. Only a death in the family exempts a Japanese family from this rigid social duty. Elsewhere, many Europeans don't use December as an occasion to distribute lengthy letters to far-flung relatives, since shorter distances tend to keep them in touch face-to-face with family and friends.

In the United States, December greetings range from the Monday-after-Thanksgiving greeting, a simply signed card that might as well declare *"Now* I can enjoy the holidays!" to the Twelfth Night family letter in early January that ruefully admits "We wish*ed* you a Merry Christmas . . ." to the annual Valentine's Day letter from a family that only comes up for air six weeks after New Year's Day. Even while people now relax about when it arrives, they put extra work into how it looks. They labor over their choice of designs, stand in line to buy just the right seasonal stamp, and even make their own pilgrimage to Bethlehem —in Maryland, Pennsylvania, or Connecticut—to capture just the right postmark.

A well-written holiday letter is a work of art to be

treasured—if only because it's all too easy to write the other kind. Every year, I receive e-mail attachments I can't open, letters that run past three single-spaced pages, descriptions of impossibly successful children, complaints about everyday aches and pains, letters from people whose names I don't recognize, and pictures of pets I've never met. Still, for every time I cringe at someone else's goofs, I remember a time when my own greetings have missed the mark. My former college adviser wrote me acerbically one year, "Thank you for the picture of your daughters and the cat. Now what are *you* doing and thinking?" Once, a recipient wrote back, "Matti died three years ago." (The year after that one, appalled, I slashed my mailing list by one-third.) I've even managed to spell *my own name* wrong. Some people send annual hopes for world peace and universal love; I just cross my fingers and hope I haven't stuck my pen in my mouth along with my foot.

I do believe that such letters are worth writing, however awkward or overblown. At holiday time, I would rather slog through a thicket of too much information, hand-drawn pictures, and amateur snapshots than survey the impersonal landscape of a beautiful commercial card with a preprinted signature that's been machine-addressed to me. I like a shaggy, friendly hug better than a cool, store-bought nod.

Even at its best, however, a holiday letter is still not everyone's cup of tea. In fact, though they may never tell you so, some of your readers place them in the same category as the dreaded fruitcake. I, however, was raised on a steady diet of homemade Christmas letters, and appreciate the ingredients that are mixed into them with such love and sincerity. And as you might predict, I love fruitcake, too.

RULES OF THUMB FOR WRITING AN ANNUAL HOLIDAY LETTER

Start early. Whatever you write will get clearer, shorter, and more expressive with several edits. Draft your letter, sleep on it, and rewrite it. Sleep on it again.

As you write, involve others. Ask your spouse to check your facts and your metaphors, and ask your children to suggest or write about what matters to them. Rather than bragging about your talented children, ask them to provide rough drafts of their news, drawings of themselves or the family, and careful signatures. Once they have helped you to stuff and stamp a holiday letter, they'll have valuable hands-on experience in how to get any letter into the mail.

Choose one overarching theme for your letter: the year of the move, the long-planned trip, your adventures in going off to college, your pleasure in your recovery, a special project, or a satisfying new hobby. Don't just list the facts; sift them and work them up into a coherent picture.

Although vivid details count, many just are not as interesting to others as they are to you. Some subjects, happy as they are, simply are not news: Most babies learn to turn over, most toddlers say cute things, and most people's daughters make beautiful brides. Add those vignettes in a few hand-written sentences to the people who would care—the aunt you named the baby after, the distant great-grandparent who doesn't see the toddler often enough, or the friend who knew the bride long ago. The passage of time is not news, either, nor is it an occasion for wonder and complaint. Routine aches and pains, the weather, and politics don't offer the reader much personal connection to your life.

Also, turn down the volume on your brag. Your family's successes are not a report card for you to flaunt. If you pat yourself on the back all the time, your friends may feel that you don't need their congratulations, too. If you just have to report on a stunning success, brag inclusively by giving it an angle that includes the reader. For example, talk about your child's hard work for a school sports award rather than your pride as a parent, or acknowledge the small disasters of the recent cross-country move as well as the glories of your new house. Talk about how you hope what you did will contribute to the world around you, not just reflect well on you.

Make your letter something your friends and family look forward to reading. Then save one copy of your letter each year for a memory book. This archive will grow to be a priceless compendium of your family's large and small recollections and achievements.

Mailing wishes for "Happy Holidays" to your friends and family should not feel like drudgery; you can slip, skimp, or skip the usual greetings.

- *Slip.* Send your greetings out after the holiday rush is over. Sending "Seasons Greetings" can celebrate the season of New Year's Day, Groundhog Day, or St. Patrick's Day with letters you have enough time to add a message to. Sending your letters later lets you answer December greetings from your more punctual friends.

- *Skimp.* Send to very few people. Triage your list to include only high-priority categories, such as people too far away to visit, people who mean the most to you, or people who have sent cards to you.

- *Skip.* That's right—don't send out any printed greetings. Lots of people don't. A newsy holiday letter alternating with a pretty card every second year might be enough.

MAKE IT PERSONAL

Make your letter look festive. Whatever format you use, lighten it up the way you brighten the outfit you'd wear to a holiday party. If you're addressing the envelopes with pen and ink, write with bright red, turquoise, or green ink. Take the time to add a holiday stamp. If you're printing a family letter, let each person's voice speak in a different font or a different color.

You can have the best of both worlds by adding hand-written notes to printed-out form letters, or send individual e-mails with attached letters. With planning, you can add personal warmth and holiday cheer to any format you use.

Every personal greeting you send by mail should have the touch of your hand somewhere. A printed return address will save you time for handwriting the recipients' addresses; printing out all your mailing-list envelopes will leave you extra time for handwritten messages. When pressed for time, I sometimes print out address labels from my mailing list but add the person's first name or initial handwritten with a colorful calligraphic flourish. This adds appeal, helps me visualize the person, shows my attention, and (I hope!) helps the person to visualize me.

CHOOSING THE RIGHT WORDS

- Include details rather than generalities: "Mamie loves her new preschool and the teachers all love her" doesn't tell as much as "Mamie carries her beloved blankie two blocks away to her preschool, in the same YMCA where all her cousins went to

This family letter hits the high points and involves the reader, with the added courtesy of arriving early in the season. Its tightly edited half-page length leaves room to add handwritten personal notes.

New address: 114 Kona Village Rd., City, HA 96087 808 282 8765

November 2009

Dear All,

Greetings again from the Kelly family in our new place, where we hope you will visit us on the "big island." There's a tiny guest room to camp out in, a nice guest cottage just down the road to rent, or resorts to splurge on nearby. We're mailing this early to update your address list so we can hear from you.

Jim's work with SolarSym brought us here; he has opened five new offices in response to the demand in Japan. Carolyn has uprooted her psychology practice, a major move for her, but she now consults part time on children's learning disabilities and finds that even in beautiful Hawaii the same problems need solving. Fred got certified in scuba and works at a dive shop, a lifelong dream he certainly couldn't pursue in Minnesota, and he takes classes in marine biology at the university. Olivia is gearing up for The Big College Search next school year; we welcome any and all suggestions.

The picture shows us surrounded by our moving boxes—still! But, you can glimpse the beautiful beach two blocks away, the palm trees, and the aqua-blue ocean. It's a warm Christmas for us, with many sunny wishes we send to you. We miss you all.

Jim Carolyn   Fred   Olivia

This all sounds a lot easier than it was! You know how much it meant to me to have your support. We hope to make it back to Edina for the big Reunion Week. We love getting your updates on Zoe's hair color . . . is she lime green now? Keep in touch and have a wonderful Xmas. ☺

THE RATIO OF JUST ENOUGH INFORMATION
TO JUST ENOUGH PEOPLE

Whether you print out your letter or attach it to an e-mail, use this rule of thumb: The longer your letter, the fewer people you should send it to. Send a half page if you mail to more than one hundred people. Send a whole page if you mail to fewer than one hundred people. Send two pages only if you limit your list to the two dozen people who know you well.

It's more important to connect warmly with a limited number of friends and family members than to dilute your efforts by over-extending yourself to include a slew of routine acquaintances. That old "can do" attitude can get you into a lot more work than you need. Be realistic about the repetitive labor involved in handwriting even a few lines to more than a small group.

Prune your mailing list twice a year: first, right after the holidays, to check whose addresses to add, remove, or change, and then again in November, to add a few more corrections and estimate how many letters to mail. Reducing the number of people you mail to will free you up to personalize what you send to the people who really count.

summer rec." A more descriptive version of "We went on a luxury cruise with great scenery and delicious food" is: "A trip down the coast of Italy took us from the canals of slowly-sinking Venice to the whitewashed cottages of Malta." If something struck you as "exotic," be specific.

- Adjectives such as *fun, fabulous, exciting, prestigious, phenomenal, successful,* and *incredible* don't give the reader anything to take pleasure in beyond your pleasure. They can shut your reader out and even cause a twinge of envy. If you can describe what it was that gave you pleasure, you'll share the benefits with the reader: the sounds and smells of the Marrakesh markets you visited, the smiling ten-year-olds at the Little League awards ceremony you attended, or the theatrical atmosphere at the dog show where Rufus won the prize for "Best Mutt."

- As you end your letter, reach out to the reader with "We miss you all," "You mean a lot to me," "I treasure my friends especially at the holidays," or "Hearing from you will mean a lot to me." Other concluding phrases are: "You are very special to us" and "Our best wishes to you and your family for the New Year, and we hope perhaps that the coming year will bring you to our door here."

CHAPTER 10

Love Letters

Do you love me or do you not,
You told me once but I forgot . . .

—Veronica Castro

To unwind on my annual Cape Cod vacation, I like to raid the local thrift store for stacks of the previous year's magazines to read in the hammock. Among the recipes for chocolate cake and the weight-loss tips, I recently came across a lovely little survey in *Women's Day* about romance. When readers were asked, "What do you want most this Valentine's Day?," more than half of them answered, "A love letter." The letter lovers' group was bigger than the next three put together: Only 20 percent chose diamond earrings, 13 percent wanted roses, and just 11 percent preferred a box of chocolates. A love letter!

Yet, in spite of how much we love to read love letters, we don't write enough of them. The quick e-mail, the evening phone call, and the text message all get the job done faster.

People who spend hours online together somehow feel too rushed to pick up a pen or wait a day for delivery.

Love letters, however, don't have to drift into the leisurely romantic past. E-mail and its digital cousins can supplement, not replace, handwritten words on paper. With the right words, timing, and materials, a love letter in any form can deliver more affection than a dozen roses.

RULES OF THUMB FOR WRITING A LOVE LETTER

Although being in love lets you feel confident of being accepted and secure in expressing your inner feelings, you can still take pleasure in treating each other with the same courtesy you give to everyone else. Whether you fell in love twenty-four hours or twenty-four years ago, always take the time to greet with warmth, spell with care, write with good grammar, and sign off with affection.

As you write, keep your funny bone next to your heart. Surveys consistently show that both men and women rate a sense of humor near the top of what made them fall in love with their soul mate.

Stay in touch with reality; while you are swearing to the truth and the whole truth, remember to limit your letter to nothing but the truth. Wild exaggeration will make everything else you write sound overblown. And bear in mind that love doesn't always last, nor does it stay in the exalted peaks of passion. It's hard enough to finesse the retraction of words you say out loud; if you have written them on paper, they are permanent, and if you have typed them in e-mail, they're fatally simple to archive and distribute. Grim but true—anything written down and signed may be used against you in a court of law, or at least the court of opinion. That's why Victorians so often signed their love letters with an initial, not their whole signature. Keep those wild promises off the page unless you are entirely sure that only your beloved will read them.

Finally, continue to write love letters throughout the years.

MAKE IT PERSONAL

This is the time for you to express yourself with sincerity and vigor. Just as you dress with extra care when you're going to spend time with each other, you can "put on" especially appealing paper, type fonts that speak for you, colors you each like best, and stamps with a shared reference.

Put extra care into picking the appropriate format for each occasion. While love inspires you to use every format you can, short of papering the walls, be sure to honor the moment with a few traditional letters handwritten on stationery. Take the time to pen a handwritten letter when you want your words to carry extra warmth and immediacy, and when they are especially worth saving. I come from a family that has saved, and eventually transcribed, the courtship letters of our great-grandparents, our grandparents, and our parents. Your own grandchildren will need something to treasure. Do you want them to find your own words in your own handwriting, or settle for commercial greeting cards and obsolete e-mail files?

Type love letters when your euphoria has calmed down. A typed document can be attached to an e-mail if you have a lot to say, want to get it exactly right, like to use nice type, and need to get it there immediately. When you rely on e-mail for daily arrangements, updates, breaking news, and reminders of your affection, you can show that you care by paying attention to your letter's grammar, spelling, and appearance. Simply enhancing the letters of her name with a different color, size, and font will remind her that she's special. Keep the subject box G-rated but specific. Remember that whatever you send to or from an office e-mail address is not guaranteed to stay private.

You already put love into writing your letter; give it a

The letter shown on the next two pages was sent to Nancy Reagan by former president Ronald Reagan. A devoted husband and natural letter writer, he writes wryly about spending their wedding anniversary alone in a hotel room away from her, but focuses mainly on his happiness and every "step toward home."

Sunday

My Darling

Here it is — our day and if we were home we'd have a fire and "funnies" and we'd hate anyone who called or dropped in.

As it is I'm sitting here on the 6th floor beside a phoney fire place looking out at a grey wet sky and listening to a radio play music not intended for one person alone.

Nevertheless I wouldn't trade the way I feel for the lonliness of those days when one place was like another and it didn't matter how long I stayed away. With all the "missing you" there is still such a wonderful warmth in the lonliness like looking forward to a bright warm room. No matter how dark &

cold it is at the moment — you know the room is there and waiting.

Of course when I say "you" anymore I'm talking a package deal — you and the two & a half year old you. Time goes so slowly and I'm such a coward when you are out of sight — so afraid something will go wrong if I'm not there to take care of you so be very careful

It's time to move on to the next town now and every move is a step toward home and you. I love you so very much I don't even mind that life made me wait so long to find you. The waiting only made the finding sweeter.

When you get this we will be almost halfway through the lonely stretch.

I love you

Ronnie

special delivery, too. Who doesn't like to find extra affection tucked in an overnight bag, a favorite book, or a lunch box? Use a "Love" stamp. Echo your message with enclosures such as flower petals, a saying from a fortune cookie, a funny photograph, or a meaningful poem.

CHOOSING THE RIGHT WORDS

- Don't hesitate to express your feelings. Some phrases to get you started are: "I woke up thinking of you," "I'm counting the [weeks, days, or hours] until we see each other again," or all-out flattery that rephrases the poetic "How do I love thee? Let me count the ways."
- Many tried-and-true words work just fine. Nobody objects to reading and rereading such sentiments as "I love you," "You are my world," and "I don't feel like myself when you are not around."
- Just as you would in a conversation, try to strike the balance between "me" and "thee" in your love letter. Write first about the two of you, next about her, and only last about yourself. For instance: "When we're together, you make me laugh like no one else" and (in reverse order) "I couldn't love you more if we were hatched from the same egg."

- Focus on the other person's strengths and appealing qualities. "I couldn't take my eyes off you from the first minute I met you" may go closer to her heart than "You are the most beautiful girl in the whole world." Although everyone likes to be thought handsome or beautiful, declarations of love should also include attention to what's inside and what you share.

- Counterintuitively, "I feel" can read better than "You are." Your beloved might prefer to hear specifically about your love for her and the happiness it brings you, rather than how generally wonderful she is.

- Give things a positive spin whenever you can. Separation can make you more appreciative of your time together: a misunderstanding can reveal the durability of your commitment, and a crisis can offer an opportunity to back each other up.

- While you're turning negatives into positives, turn those neutrals into superlatives with a touch of humor. Look for the figure of speech that sums up, with a smile, your love and your beloved: "You're the croutons in my salad" or "When the silver lining turns out to be a cloud, you're my red umbrella."

CHAPTER 11

Breakup Letters

I'm writing you a dear John letter,
I tried to stay but it never got better.

—*"Dear John Letter," by Dwight Reynolds, Kevin Briggs, Patrice Stewart,*
and Whitney Houston, 2002

When you have fallen out of love, it's tempting just to junk the whole past along with the present and future, and to lower your own standards about what you say to this once-beloved person. When Mr. Right has morphed into Dear John, writing a civilized letter enables you to take the high road, setting the tone for a merciful and orderly dismantling of the relationship.

The breakup letter belongs to a long, honorable tradition of explaining why a connection is finished, reaching from the American Declaration of Independence, to Che Guevara's farewell letter to Castro and the Cuban Revolution, to the breakup by Post-it note in *Sex and the City*. A personal letter helps you to make the best exit from a dead-end street. It lets you treat humanely someone you used to care about, while you salvage your dignity, disconnect the connection, and get on with your own life.

RULES OF THUMB FOR WRITING A BREAKUP LETTER

Plan to write a draft first, and then sleep on it, just to make sure you won't regret what you've written.

As you write, be short, specific, and decisive. Follow the age-old political advice of "Never complain, never explain, never apologize." These just open the door to rehashing the past rather than moving forward.

Your tone should be kind and civil. Acknowledge briefly that you used to feel one way and now you feel differently. It's important to be honest, if it's really over. Don't include the false hope that your feelings might be rekindled.

Also, put away your poison pen. If you are not just breaking up but divorcing, don't put specific accusations, threats, apologies, confessions, or promises on paper. Don't write anything to your spouse or your ex that could sour his relationship with your children if they were to read it. Remember that anything you put on paper or in an e-mail could end up in the wrong hands. An ex with a grudge can send your letter around to make you look bad.

Remind your former love that in putting this behind you, you are destroying his letters and deleting all of his e-mails. Encourage him to do the same. That helps both of you accept that neither of you will cling to reminders from the past.

At the conclusion of your letter, be clear about what you think should come next, if you know your own mind. Avoid prolonging the agony by proposing to stay friends, although that may evolve on its own later. Be positive about him and his future. This reassures him that you still think that he is a good man and that he can find someone else who will fully appreciate him. Just not you.

MAKE IT <u>LESS</u> PERSONAL

This is the one personal letter that should be *less* personal. You don't exactly want to compose a legal document, but you can make use of what you know about warming a personal letter up to cool this one down. You can even type and print it out to emphasize that you are aiming for an arm's-length relationship.

This letter, coming at the end of a lot of other communication, tries to put an end to the dialogue and the relationship. The writer deliberately chooses an impersonal printout letter in a plain font style to give a chilly tone of finality, and she uses a large point size to make it more assertive (small type can seem meek and uncertain). She even adds her signature in type.

10-2-09

Dear John,

I hope you can read this letter in the spirit I write it. I'm just telling you again, this time on paper, that it's really over between us. No matter how much you talk it around and around, you and I want different things from life and from this relationship. I know I do, and I don't expect to change my mind.

You've tried and tried to make it work, but it's just *not going to work*. Please stop calling me and arguing about it. I will send you the rest of your stuff in ten days, as soon as I pack up. Please don't e-mail me, either. You'll just get the same answer.

Thanks for some good years, and for accepting that they are now really part of the past.

Good luck,

Emily

Make your letter forceful even as you make it less personal. The breakup letter on paper offers you the great advantage of a classy solo performance to a captive audience of one. You can showcase your convictions without being interrupted or challenged. If your soon-to-be ex then telephones or confronts you in person, you now have the letter to fall back on as your mission statement, a document that feels much more permanent than any rebuttal by e-mail or "Yeah, but . . ." that you stammer out loud.

Choose cool, plain, impersonal colors and paper—no stark, legalistic black and white but also no cute, friendly touches. Don't write when you're upset—your handwriting will look awful and you'll use words you might need to eat later. Deliver your letter by hand, or by mail if you're already seeing each other only now and then.

If you can't face saying good-bye in person, don't take the coward's way out by doing it electronically. Put it on paper. Breaking up solely by e-mail dishonors the importance of the feelings you once believed in. It also encourages instant, effortless arguments in reply, and draws you into a Ping-Pong match of single-sentence dialogue. And never, ever break up by text message. It's tacky and cowardly.

CHOOSING THE RIGHT WORDS

- You can start out with the standard "Dear John," salutation without implying much affection. To be more abrupt, simply greet him with his name, "John," without the "Dear." It's uncivil, but it may be needed to lower the temperature.
- Use the pronouns *I* and *you* rather than *we.*
- Use direct statements like "It's over," "I don't want to spend any more time with you," and "There's no way to make this work."
- Don't keep engaging in arguments and accusations. "You always" and "You never" will keep the two of you locked in an unwinnable battle, where you're still connected.
- Limit your closing to something noncommittal like "Regards" or "Sincerely" or "Good luck" or "Best wishes" rather than the warmer "Yours" or "Love." Closing with "I wish you well" emphasizes that you two are not "we" any longer and now face two separate paths.

CHAPTER 12

Letters to Say "Can We Try Again?"

No matter what I say or do
There's just no getting over you.
—Natalie Cole, "Miss You Like Crazy," 1989

When you would like to get back together with a former love, you need a letter that combines an apology, an invitation, a request for help, and a valentine. Your choice of format, materials, and wording—even how you choose to send the letter—should all deliver a message of sincerity and low-key pressure.

It's important to strike the right tone when you are interested in renewing a relationship. You're sticking your neck out. You have to show an honest desire to connect but protect your pride if you don't succeed.

Now aren't you glad you wrote that classy breakup letter? A letter can reopen the door to being a couple again if you didn't slam it on your way out. As the old prayer says,

"Dear Lord, make my words always soft and tender, because later I may have to eat them."

RULES OF THUMB FOR WRITING A "TRY AGAIN" LETTER

Ask yourself what you can realistically hope to accomplish and then make sure your letter focuses on that. Do you just want to be friends, do you want to meet for coffee to talk about some remaining unresolved issue like ownership of the book collection, or do you want to reset the clock to a happier time and try to go forward together as a couple? Are you just curious about what's going on in your ex's life? If you know what you want, you can signal what kind of response you hope to hear. Often the best goal for a "try again" letter is to get together in person as soon as you can.

If you want to reopen any interrupted conversation, don't start off with a windy monologue. Keep it succinct. Break the text up into reasonable paragraphs; otherwise, it may look like an angry outburst or an unhinged ramble. As always, don't drink and write.

Write about your own feelings, suitably toned down, without trying to second-guess hers. Don't write this letter if you just want to dredge up old grudges or spread more blame. In fact, don't try to justify anything by blaming her or pleading for amnesty. As the French say, *"Qui s'excuse, s'accuse,"* or "He who excuses himself, accuses himself." Eat a small serving of crow in claiming partial responsibility for the split. But don't assume that just writing "I'm sorry" will magically let the two of you start over fresh; be ready for potential indifference or hostility.

Frame your letter in terms of the future you might have again together, whether as friends or a couple, but don't go too far toward reopening the old romance, in case she has completely moved on. Try to find a balance between warmth and caution; she's probably going to feel flattered to some degree at being remembered and wanted, whether she's actually interested or not.

MAKE IT PERSONAL

You know this person well, maybe too well. Choose a format for your letter that lets her see that you want to try to cooperate with her, not to confront and oppose her, have the last word, or trivialize the problem that caused your breakup.

Mind your manners. Don't use notebook paper, sta-

An old flame gets back in touch with a friendly, low-key letter, testing the water before plunging in. He writes with enough eagerness to show real interest, but he doesn't sound pushy.

4321 GREENWOOD DRIVE, WINNETKA ILL. 76548
22 APRIL 2009

DEAR ALISON,

I WAS REMINDED OF YOU WHEN I HEARD
A RADIO PROGRAM ABOUT HIGH SCHOOL YEARBOOKS.
LOTS OF GOOD MEMORIES CAME BACK,
INCLUDING WHAT YOU WROTE IN MY BOOK
FOUR YEARS AGO. REMEMBER? I HOPE
YOU DON'T MIND MY WRITING TO YOU. I KNOW
WE LEFT A LOT OF THINGS UP IN THE AIR,
AND THAT'S BOTHERED ME FOR A LONG TIME.

I'VE BEEN WONDERING WHAT YOU WENT ON
TO DO AFTER YOU MOVED AWAY. I WAS
MARRIED FOUR YEARS, NOW BACK ON MY OWN,
WORKING FOR THE FIRM THAT USED TO RENOVATE
FOR MY UNCLE. AFTER A YEAR IN MADISON,
I'M LIVING NEAR CHICAGO.

IF YOU'D LIKE TO GET TOGETHER, I'M AVAILABLE.
I'LL BE IN YOUR NEIGHBORHOOD SEEING OLD
FRIENDS SATURDAY AND SUNDAY MAY 2-3.
ARE YOU FREE FOR DINNER OR LUNCH? COFFEE?
YES OR NO. IT WILL BE GOOD JUST TO HEAR
FROM YOU.

YOURS AS EVER,
BILL

tionery with your office letterhead, or a casual postcard.
Use good but not opulent materials. Make your letter well
dressed but not stuffy. If you were both habitual e-mail writers, keep your handwritten letter brief and informal; if you
both used to be comfortable on paper, write a page or two.
If your letter is successful, it may just be the one you will
laugh over and your grandchildren will treasure.

A printout letter won't seem personal enough unless
you type a few sentences and then continue in handwriting.
Hand-address the envelope.

If she has relocated, you can request her new address by
e-mail and ask if you might write her a letter. Don't try to
put too much eloquence into the dry e-mail format.

Your choice of delivery sets the stage. You can prop
your letter on her desk at work, send it special delivery, attach it to a dozen roses, or just drop it into an old-fashioned
postbox. Ask yourself what message each form of delivery
sends. Will an envelope under her door after a monthlong
separation warm her heart or creep her out? Try to picture
whether her first reaction will be a fond "Aw . . ." or an
eye-rolling "Ick!"

CHOOSING THE RIGHT WORDS

- Use "I'm sorry" to refer to splitting up, not to any
  specific thing (especially something you think she

did) that may have caused it. That's a topic for later or never.

- To avoid seeming needy or sounding like a stalker, don't use words that demand attention. Scary phrases may include "I want" or "I need" or "We have to talk."

- Don't overuse *I* and *you;* focus on writing thoughts that include *we.*

- Don't whine. "You hurt my feelings," or "You owe me an apology," or "I'm still reeling from that heartless e-mail" won't help your effort to become a couple again.

CHAPTER 13

Letters of Congratulation

Flatter me, and I may not believe you. Criticize me,
and I may not like you. Ignore me, and I may not forgive you.
Encourage me, and I will not forget you.

—Pastor, scholar, and author William Arthur Ward (1921–1994)

ords on paper make the best pat on the back. Although many people's lives are filled with more than enough gifts and parties, most still hunger for the personal words of their friends and family to help them celebrate a birth, graduation, marriage, or achievement. Your personal letter of congratulation can add something unique to any event. Whatever the milestone, don't let it pass by without writing a personal letter.

In every life, there are a few happy occasions when people like to stop, gather their friends around them, and enjoy the fruits of their work, their luck, and their endurance. Take the time to praise achievement with words rather than prizes, whether a child is excelling in school, winning at sports, or has earned an award for "most improved player." Adults enjoy recognition just as much—for promotions or retirement, the publication of a book, or the completion of a marathon.

Other, more formal events also call for a letter of congratulation: a birthday, a wedding, or a major anniversary. Finally, sometimes people deserve recognition just for hanging in there. If you wrap your encouragement in congratulations, you help your reader feel more like a conquering hero than a struggling underdog.

Congratulating people for their successes, it turns out, will strengthen your relationships even more than consoling people for their woes. A recent study in the *Journal of Personality and Social Psychology* reports that people felt worse when their achievements were greeted without enthusiasm than they did when their problems were minimized. "You get much more bang for your buck by amplifying life's rewards than by soothing its bruises," says Dr. Shelly Gable. So don't just say "Way to go!" out loud in a crowd—write it in a personal letter.

RULES OF THUMB FOR WRITING A LETTER OF CONGRATULATION

Mention the happy occasion, the honorees, and the date and place, and emphasize the importance of the milestone. Include specific details about the person and the event.

Congratulate people for their intentions, hard work,

or perseverance, not just their good luck. (A retirement or a major birthday is partly about effort, but it's also about fortitude.) Congratulate children appropriately, emphasizing their effort rather than their fame, their deservingness rather than their luck, their pride more than yours. A well-written letter of congratulation adds to their long-term understanding of the civilized use of the written word.

When sending anniversary wishes to a couple, your letter should be about each of them, their relationship with each other, the occasion, your relationship with them, and connections in general. Tell them how much you value the connection you all share.

MAKE IT PERSONAL

The format for a letter of congratulation should match the important nature of the message. Show that you've put in effort to celebrate his achievement. A handwritten or printout letter reflects the permanence and effort of the occasion. Although congratulations conveyed by e-mail or telephone can deliver the initial "hurrah," they don't compare to a tangible letter. Commemorate an achievement by writing a keepsake.

Choose materials that, depending on the event, look festive and bright or elegant and formal. A thirtieth birthday, for example, can feature a brightly colored poster-size proclamation, whereas a fortieth anniversary calls for more sedate, formal stationery. A letter from a favorite aunt to a two-year-old birthday girl for her keepsake chest can pull out all the stops with Beatrix Potter stationery and fanciful writing. Whatever paper you use should be durable, because your letter may be archived to be read again in the future.

MEMORY BOOKS

Letters of congratulation can be collected in a memory book, sometimes known by its German name—*festschrift,* or "celebration writing"—to be presented in public recognition or assembled privately by the person himself. If you want to organize this kind of book, contact the contributors far ahead of time and suggest the letter format, length, and deadline. (Decide whether the letters' tone and wording are to be for the reader only or for everyone to share.) The memory book makes a perfect present for people who, in later years, do not need or want a table full of gifts or a stack of greeting cards. It makes a perfect present to celebrate a retirement, a major anniversary, or an eightieth birthday.

If your handwriting is not up to the task of a full-page letter, then print out your words, changing the default font so your letter won't look like anyone else's. Sign it with a flourish, and if your signature is hard to read, spell out your whole name on a separate line.

16 Semaphore Road.
Guildford.
10th September, 1951.

Dear Derrick
                You will be entering
a new School tomorrow so I write
to wish much happiness & great
success in it. You will continue
to work diligently.

    I am very glad that I had the
privilege of having you in our
school & shall have pleasant
& grateful recollections of your genial
manners & willing help at all times.

    I shall always be glad to hear
of your progress so come & see us
often especially if you have any
difficulty with your studies.

        My very kind regards & best wishes.

            Yours very sincerely
            John Gardiner

CHOOSING THE RIGHT WORDS

- Write words of congratulation in the most upbeat phrases you can repeat or think up. Don't edge into his spotlight by saying "I'm so proud of you," and don't use the words *jealous* or *envious*. His special moment is not about you.

- Congratulate him on the recent past and the happy moment while also predicting a bright future. Be sure that you include the phrases "You will . . ." or "I will . . ." or "It will . . ." in your letter.

- Feel free to use the standard words of praise, since most people don't mind being congratulated, complimented, and admired: "Well done," "You did it!," and "Great work!"

- Keep going after you've said "Congratulations!" Single out something special to add—a memory of an early and deserving effort, an overheard compliment, or an extra insight.

- Close with a reminder that you value your relationship, and sign off with the warmest and most positive closing you know. "Warmly," "In celebration," "Fondly," "Bravo" or "Brava."

An Englishman in his seventies still treasures a letter that he received from his headmaster congratulating him on being accepted to the local grammar school.

CHAPTER 14

Letters of Condolence

*Yet, taught by time, my heart has learned to glow
For other's good, and melt at other's woe.*

—Homer ("Smyrns of Chios"), the Odyssey, translated by Alexander Pope

The verb *condole* comes from two words that mean "with" and "feel pain." When you write a letter of condolence, you share feelings of sadness with a person who is grieving the death of a loved one, while you affirm the importance of the loss. You also reflect on the good things you appreciated about the person who has died and the connection that you shared. (In the chapter that follows this one, you will find guidance on how to write a letter of sympathy for other kinds of loss and misfortune less devastating than death.)

Send words of comfort, in some form, to the bereaved person right away—either in an e-mail or a short note during the first week or in a handwritten note within two weeks, or send both. A telephone call to express condolence is not in the same league with words on paper. It could interrupt the bereaved, may not even be remembered, and certainly can't be reread. If, after the initial grief and shock, you write again, you can focus more on celebrating the person's life and dwell less on feeling bereft. Long after the flowers that give comfort at a funeral have wilted, the letters that you send will be read and reread for years.

RULES OF THUMB FOR WRITING A LETTER OF CONDOLENCE

Follow the traditional letter format by opening with warm greetings to the chief mourner. If there is no obvious chief mourner, address the person you know best.

The text of a letter of condolence should include these parts, in roughly this order:

- Acknowledge the loss specifically without using euphemisms such as "passed away."
- Express your sympathy.
- Mention special qualities of the deceased beyond generic words of praise. Write about the person's life, not her death. Describe cherished details.
- Add a specific happy memory of the person who has died. Cite something that connects the two of you if possible.
- If you live nearby and are writing within the first

week (or if you send a preliminary e-mail), suggest
some specific tasks you could help with, such as
calling a list of people, housing a visitor, meeting a
train, or picking up take-out food, rather than just
offer "anything I can do."

Show that the survivor's loss and the deceased person's
life are both still in your thoughts, and calibrate your condolence to the bereaved person's progress. For instance, if
you are writing after a few months, one widower may have
already moved on and remarried, whereas another may still
be stuck deep in unresolved grief. Don't assume too much
about the progress of a person's grief; it may be worse or
better than what you think.

Focus on connections: between you and the person
who died, you and the bereaved, and all of you (family and
friends) in support of the survivors.

In your concluding sentences, ask to have your letter's
sentiments passed along to other mourners, such as the deceased person's siblings, spouse, or colleagues.

Finally, don't expect to get it all down in one sitting.
Write things you remember in a rough draft and then sleep
on it, so you don't leave out something especially nice.

MAKE IT PERSONAL

Use your own words. Don't buy a commercial card with someone else's words printed in someone else's calligraphy.

Some families hold memorial services months after the funeral itself. For a thoughtful overview of a person's life to be added to a family's collection of tributes, a typed letter that you print out on business-size personal stationery may suit the occasion's formality.

Never send a serious condolence letter by e-mail, except as an attached document (described above) or when mail delivery is difficult. A study by the Pilot pen company in the 1990s revealed that while many people may have sent such condolence letters themselves, when asked how they would feel about receiving one, nearly 75 percent said they would be hurt.

The colors you choose should look subdued and soothing, but not stark—blue ink on cream paper, for instance, is visually softer than black ink on white paper. Put a "Love" stamp on the envelope; you can count on its availability from the post office every year.

CHOOSING THE RIGHT WORDS

- Write the person's name. Don't refer to her as "the departed."

July 31, 1997

Dear Geoffrey

Thank you so much for sending us the article about your mother's life and death. What a remarkable person Eleanor was! We feel so lucky to have known her. And thanks, too, for using the Hopi picture. When your mother and dad visited us in Arizona all of us had a marvelous time exploring a museum of Hopi culture.

We weren't the only people who loved her visits and her letters. She gave the nicest talk to my club about the textiles she had collected over the years from the many places they traveled to. I know how much you missed her, but she gave joy to people wherever she went. Also she always had letters and pictures from you to show us plus interesting tales to tell.

And thank you for keeping her in touch with her friends during the past twelve years when she couldn't write for herself. I know that time was hard for her and for you. Please convey to your sisters how much we all will miss her.

Yours,
Jane and Stan

- Warm words to use include: *remember, memory, life, comfort, death, loss, miss, missed, shared, valued,* and *together.*
- Don't overuse the following words: *sad, sorry, grieve, mourn, alone, lonely,* or *gone.*
- Never write "I know how you feel," "I feel," "You'll feel better," "It's better this way," "I'm upset," "I don't know what to say," or "It's awful." Don't compare your own grief with hers.
- Keep your closing warm and positive: "Your friend," "Love," "With a warm hug," "Yours," "Affectionately yours," "Very sincerely," "With my deepest sympathy," or "Fondly."

This condolence letter comes from an old friend on the occasion of the death of an eighty-five-year-old. It focuses both on the past and on recent years, mentioning places, relationships, and visual details.

CHAPTER 15

Letters of Sympathy

*True sympathy is putting ourselves in another's place; and we
are moved in proportion to the reality of our imagination.*

—American clergyman Hosea Ballou (1771–1852)

All of us suffer occasional disasters that leave us walking but wounded. As a friend or relative, you can give a boost to anyone who has lost a job, had a child in trouble, been a victim of a crime, lost a competition, failed a challenge, split up with a spouse, faced a major disappointment, or just encountered an uphill trudge when he had hoped for a downhill run.

Words of sympathy will bring more comfort if you send some of them in writing rather than say them all out loud. People who are facing adversity have days when they are down and days when they are up. On the wrong day, clichés that assure them that they are strong enough to manage— "You can do it"—may be the last thing they want to read. On the right day, your words can give them something substantial to lean on. Reading your letter without you there may make it easier for them to absorb your words when they feel ready to hear them.

RULES OF THUMB FOR WRITING A LETTER OF SYMPATHY

Keep your tone respectful and kind, rather than offhand or informal. Let people decide for themselves if they want to keep a stiff upper lip.

Don't wring your hands and catastrophize. That's their job, in private. Strike a tone between being unrealistically upbeat and hopelessly maudlin. Commiseration should include faith in the other person's ability to keep going, but you should refrain from being relentlessly perky.

Finally, remember that suggestions are not always the same thing as help. Don't offer unsolicited advice unless you have truly been in the other person's circumstances—and even then only if you are certain that he would find your ideas useful. Wait to be asked.

MAKE IT PERSONAL

Choose the format for your letter that suits the length and breadth of the misfortune: perhaps a sympathetic e-mail for a passing slump, and a one page handwritten letter for

the death of a beloved pet. Consider the best form of delivery, also. For instance, it may be best to hand-deliver
a brief, general supportive letter to the home of a crime
victim when you come by to help.

When offering sympathy, the sooner, the shorter. Write
a quick note immediately to show general support, and a
longer letter if appropriate, after the dust has settled a bit.

Send an e-mail with your encouragement and specific
suggestions for a job search, if you actually have useful information, not just random bright ideas. This keeps the tone
brisk and businesslike, rather than grave and personal. Type
a document to mail or attach it to an e-mail when you write
detailed material such as contact information, if you're sure
this really will help. Offer to make phone calls or write a
letter of recommendation, but refrain from urging your advice on someone who may already be overwhelmed with
sorting out offers of assistance.

The style of the materials that you choose for a letter of
sympathy should not be too stark and bracing nor too sweet
and sappy. Take your cues from the reader. If you're confident he would respond well to a sunny, energizing piece of
mail, send that. Otherwise, take a more conservative approach, but don't be so severe that your letter of comfort
just underscores your friend's depressing experience.

From: Aunt Clara
To: Callie
Subject: Better days have GOT to come soon
Date: March 17, 2008

Dear Callie,

I'm so sorry to hear that Fernando is having a rocky time settling in to his first month in Phoenix. He's such a <u>noticer</u>—he pays attention to things the rest of us miss—so it must be overwhelming for him to absorb his new house, new neighborhood, new baby brother, new friends, and new school. Five is such an opinionated age, too. (A lot like forty!)

I wish I could be nearby to offer some real help. But it sounds like you have a handle on it and that it is already beginning to get better. I'm sending a small box off to all three boys tomorrow with some souvenirs from last summer's get-together (including those snapshots, plus a puzzle he seemed to enjoy) and an empty frame for him to start collecting pictures of his new friends.

All my love and a big hug,
Aunt Clara

A sympathetic e-mail letter is appropriate in a rapidly evolving situation, when a letter would take too long to arrive and an attachment would be too formal. A friendly font can warm up the standard e-mail type.

CHOOSING THE RIGHT WORDS

- Say "I feel for you," "I'm thinking of you," "I hope things get better," "I'm sure," and "You're in my thoughts."
- Don't say "Cheer up," "This will pass," "Don't cry," "Anything I can do?," "It's just awful," "Don't feel bad," "I'm shocked" (it's not about you), or "I know how you feel." Don't allude to your own troubles.
- If you write "Call me if you need anything," follow that phrase with two or three specific things you'd like to help with and ask the reader to choose. Make it easy for him to ask.
- Use your imagination. If you were in this situation, would you like to hear "This is just awful," "What a disaster!," "Well, I'm not surprised," and "I lived through it, so you will, too," or, rather, "This may take some time, but it sounds like you're doing the right thing"?
- If you use euphemisms (such as "your situation"), you may make future discussion of the reader's problem taboo. Try to avoid them.

CHAPTER 16

Letters to Someone
Who Is Ill

The I in illness is isolation,
and the crucial letters in wellness are we.

—*As quoted in Mimi Guarneri,* The Heart Speaks: A Cardiologist Reveals
the Secret Language of Healing, *2006*

*S*ympathy takes a special form when you write to someone who is suffering from an illness or injury. Some
patients who are bedridden for even a short time report that
they receive way too many flowers and not enough ink on
paper. When the impulse strikes you to buy a card or send
a bouquet, you should add—or substitute—a good long
letter that they can read and reread.

RULES OF THUMB FOR WRITING
TO SOMEONE WHO IS ILL

Check with caregivers, family, and hospital staff to find out
what type of letter is best for the patient to read and possi-

bly to answer. Rather than handle a flood of e-mails, phone calls, and messages, families with a person in a health crisis often designate one member as the contact person, or set up a central Web site where people can check for updates.

Especially at first, and for all patients with serious health problems, route your communications through these care-givers and relatives, who will know the best way for you to write to the person and to get updates on medical news. For the same reason, don't assume that what you write is con-fidential; it may be read out loud to the patient by someone else, and passed around or displayed.

Be upbeat and encouraging. If you pray for people, tell them so; even most atheists don't object to other people's prayers.

What you're thinking is often of great interest to some-one shut in or separated from you. What you're feeling, though, may be too much for her to deal with. And your worries and problems are not something you should ask her to contemplate with her limited reserve of emotional energy. Therefore, don't add your own moods to the sick person's very real problems. Don't try to trump her suffer-ing with your own little peeves and past illnesses.

Whatever the situation, you should make your friend feel as if she is still part of the outside world. The routines of ordinary life give a sense of self that is disconcertingly absent for the sick; reassure her that she is still very present in people's thoughts.

Finally, follow up any visit or conversation with some thoughts on paper.

MAKE IT PERSONAL

Within the guidelines that caregivers have provided, use any form of communication you can for staying in touch, from a sticky note on a book you are mailing to an e-mail to be printed out and read aloud.

If you send a purchased "get well" card, add at least three handwritten sentences of your own. Although a short handwritten note reminds her that you're thinking of her, it won't convey much of what you're thinking. Your full-length letter, on the other hand, will create your virtual presence at her bedside. Put plenty into it.

Write on sunny and cheerful stationery or cards. A picture makes a nice enclosure, and a clipping with news may be more engaging than your secondhand report of it.

Some people who can sit up may still lack the energy to round up writing materials and addresses or to find someone to be a gofer. Make it extra easy for the person to reply by enclosing stationery, a pen, and stamped envelopes pre-addressed to you and to some other people who are important to the patient. If you think this type of enclosure will seem demanding, make it humorous.

March 11, 2008,

Dear Kamilla,

I hope this finds you feeling better & sitting up. Jack said you were doing major physical therapy — what a strenuous full time job. But good for you (and your doctor) for getting your leg bending again right away. I know you'll do a good job at PT. Anyone who could keep showing up for crew all winter at 6 AM can certainly ace PT. I hear there are beautiful walks laid out around the Center, so you have something to enjoy when you get up to hobble around.

I'd love to come visit & bring you a care package from the outside world. What do you hanker for? Fruit? Magazines? Music? Comic relief? Call me at 555-460-1019 or drop this postcard in the mail to me in case it's hard to get to a phone or e. mail. Sarita has been asking how to visit you, so if you'd like me to give her a ride over just let me know. Or if you're just too over-whelmed we can wait.   Love, Katya

CHOOSING THE RIGHT WORDS

- In setting a positive tone, make sure you deal with reality. "Get well quickly," "I hope you feel better soon," "We wish you a speedy recovery," or "Be out of bed soon," or even words to the effect of "Get well slowly," are welcome words when recovery is a real possibility. If, however, a person is only, inevitably, headed for worse health and knows it, then some form of "Feel better" or "Hang in there" is more appropriate.
- Ban the words *upset* and *awful* from your vocabulary. Don't say "I feel."
- Don't write words that undermine the patient's confidence in the doctor's diagnosis or treatment. As a young George Washington wrote in his *Rules of Civility & Decent Behaviour in Company and Conversation*, ". . . do not Presently play the Physicion if you be not Knowing therein." Or even if you be!

A neighbor writes to a patient in a long-term recovery from an accident, acknowledging the seriousness of the situation, focusing on the reader's abilities, and offering specific help. She makes it easy to reply.

CHAPTER 17

Letters of Advice

> *You cannot teach a man anything;*
> *you can only help him find it within himself.*
>
> —Galileo Galilei (1564–1642)

A personal letter offers the best way to give advice, if you write it with care. It allows you to think through what you want to say and then word it clearly, and it lets your reader absorb your suggestions in private before responding. However, while you are writing the letter, you hear only your own voice, with no one's feedback to warn you if you stray from being warm and helpful to being strident and preachy. The reader may misread something you've written or take offense at your tone, and he may overreact by tuning out the whole message—and any subsequent advice you offer. The good news is that you can learn to use the letter's strengths to avoid its pitfalls so that your well-meant advice will be well received.

If you're lucky enough to be asked for advice, it's easy

to compose an answer. You know what tone to take, you've been directed toward a topic to cover, and you know that the letter will be welcome. Remember, though, that people asking for advice may simply want to open a conversation and might even argue with you, testing their ideas by expressing them to someone they trust. You'll both learn from the dialogue. As playwright Brendan Behan observed, "People who ask our advice almost never take it. Yet we should never refuse to give it, upon request, for it often helps us to see our own way more clearly."

Quite often, people who may need your advice don't have the inclination to ask for it. In these instances, you may find that writing your advice in a carefully worded letter works better than speaking it out loud. I've occasionally written—sometimes typed and revised—letters like this to people I already see every day, when I just couldn't find the right occasion to discuss a teenager's spending habits or explain the reasons behind some disputed house rule.

Sometimes the written letter is the very best tool for personal change. Experts in substance abuse, for example, place great trust in the personal letter as a method for intervening in a crisis. Whether you hope to make a major transformation in someone's life or just map out a new set of rules about what your child's allowance will cover, it's easier to start from and stick to words you've written on paper. And advice on paper may be easier for some people to read, accept, and act on than even the most tactful advice in person.

If nothing else, including your advice lets you go on record about your belief. When Abigail Adams urged her husband in a 1776 letter to "remember the ladies," she may not have influenced any of the laws he drafted, but she did give voice to women then and now who have been encouraged by her advocacy.

RULES OF THUMB FOR WRITING A LETTER OF ADVICE

As the old saying goes, if you have to eat a live frog, it's best not to look at him too long. Don't let things that you genuinely need to write get bottled up; write while you're still thinking rather than feeling.

Before you begin your letter, weigh your advice in the larger scheme of things and factor in the possible side effects your dose of advice may produce: offending the person, using up your ammunition (you can give advice only once in a while), and picking an already-lost battle.

The classic steps for solving any problem include one vital preliminary step: *Be sure there is a problem.* Sometimes people alienate each other by trying to change a situation that turns out not to exist. For example, before you send your nephew a list of colleges you think he should apply to, check around to make sure he's not way ahead of you. People don't generally like to be told to do something they've already planned to do themselves.

Ask yourself, Am I the right person to deliver this message? Don't give advice that should come from someone else.

In addition, don't deliver major advice on small matters or write a whole letter on a complaint that can be better resolved in person, such as a comment you disliked or an assumption you question. Don't bring up your own reactions. Don't drag in your annoyance, worry, anger, and embarrassment. People seldom welcome advice about how they should feel or how they should change what they are doing to make you feel better. When you have solved the part of the situation that each of you can control, then problems about your feelings will solve themselves.

While you stay courteous and calm, be consistent, persistent, and insistent. Stick to your message. Don't spread out from your target topic to deliver a general barrage of *should*s. As you write, describe the reader's conduct in the best terms. Convey your good intentions when you suggest that he change what he does, and always give him a chance to explain or reply.

Write, or at least draft and sleep on, a difficult letter before dread and exasperation weaken your resolve or build up to an outburst. Getting something off your chest will be easier if you remind yourself that you don't actually have to send the letter until you've toned it down. Often, simply writing it helps you get your feelings out of the foreground.

You won't always get a reply or see an immediate change.

November 2, 2002

Dear Cassie,

How good it was to have that afternoon visit with you last weekend! Thanks for coming out on such a rainy day. We loved seeing you all.

I do admire the calm way you are handling Nathan's big year of college searches. But sometimes when you worry in front of him about his grades and chances, it seems to make him uncomfortable. He's such a sensitive kid. I wouldn't even mention it, except that you're usually so considerate of other people's feelings.

I'm still sensitized to this issue, from watching Lizzie struggle with her own applications last year. You remember? I found that I just had to let her take charge of the whole process — mistakes and all. The best help one can give is at the lowest level: addresses, stamps, deadlines, minor edits.

This nervous time creates stress for any teenager and any family. I'd love to help by driving Nathan to his Friday appointments, since I pass right by that building anyway. And please ask me for anything else that might lighten some of the commuting for you.

With love and affection,

Jane

In a letter, the poet Edna St. Vincent Millay wrote, "Please give me some good advice in your next letter. I promise not to follow it." The person may act on your advice years later, or never, but at least by writing a thoughtful letter you will have the satisfaction of going on record with the kind of clarity that daily nagging just doesn't convey.

MAKE IT PERSONAL

The format that you choose for your letter can make a difference to the reader's acceptance. The daily informality of e-mail, for instance, can sometimes prevent your advice from seeming confrontational and can make it feel more like a natural part of an ongoing conversation. Many people check their e-mail often and find it easier to anwer than snail mail. This format can, however, make your message sound blunt or mundane. Use it for minor topics.

A printed letter, in contrast, helps you get the wording just right, and it also cools down some of the direct, conversational intimacy that can transpire in an e-mail exchange. Sometimes that makes the whole situation less agitated.

One sister writes to another with support during a stressful year. She makes an easy-to-accept offer to take care of a small chore, opening the door to a better insight into other ways to help later on. Her handwriting keeps the tone friendly, not officious, and yet affirms the topic's importance.

Finally, a handwritten letter lays your relationship on the line, making you seem very present in the reader's imagination. If the personal urgency of a long handwritten letter of advice makes the reader feel overwhelmed, though, he may back off or tune you out. Send a handwritten letter only when you and the reader are closely connected, when he is familiar already with your handwriting, and when the matter means a lot to you.

CHOOSING THE RIGHT WORDS

- Sandwich one slice of criticism carefully between two compliments, and garnish it with an offer of help. For example, you can write a three-paragraph letter along these lines: "I think you both are handling Chuck's injury stoically. But sometimes when you argue about his exercise program, it makes people uncomfortable. It just doesn't sound like you, since you've stayed so cheerful in the midst of all the uproar."

- Avoid writing "You always," "You never," "I hate to say this," "Why don't you," "If I were you," "No offense," and "I know you don't want my advice, but."

- Make your advice as low-key as you can. Soften

accusations down to complaints, complaints down to suggestions, and suggestions down to comments. If you must criticize, tone it down. "Help me understand this" is better than "Why do you always do this?"

CHAPTER 18

Letters to Ask for Help

The healthy, the strong individual,
is the one who asks for help when he needs it,
whether he has an abscess on his knee or in his soul.

—Columnist Rona Barrett

From time to time, we all need to request help—for an introduction, a favor, advice, or just a place to sleep. When you ask for help in person, you put people on the spot. If there's the slightest chance they'll say yes while their gut says no, or turn you down in a hurry when time to think would have let them convince themselves to say yes, write a letter instead. By asking on paper or in an e-mail, you can create a period of grace for them to think over your request before answering. Your letter also shows that you have put effort of your own into asking them for their effort.

Planning ahead is of the highest importance in your request for help. As the author of a dozen books about how to do calligraphy, I have files filled with the hand-scrawled requests I receive—sometimes in pencil on torn-out note-book paper—from high-school students who have left their research paper on calligraphy until the last minute: "Can you tell me in a few sentences what is the message of your books?" "Can you write me a long paragraph in answer to these ten questions?" "I need to hear back by Monday with a suggested list of books." Although I would never insult or discourage any young person who writes a letter, I do try to use these eleventh-hour requests as a teachable moment when I reply. I usually answer just a few of their questions, and suggest they practice looking things up in an author's books rather than asking the author directly.

Wanting help is not a sign of weakness or an admission that you cannot cope. People *like* to be asked, and they like to help. Most of us, in fact, feel friendlier toward someone we can help than toward the paragon of independence who takes pride in never needing anything we can offer.

RULES OF THUMB FOR WRITING A LETTER OF REQUEST FOR HELP

Keep your letter succinct, preferably on one side of one page. Explain the situation to your reader, request help, and describe the plan that requires her specific assistance. Mention why you are asking her and not someone else. A clear, courteous request for specific help, worded so that the person you ask can comfortably say no, will save her from having to read your mind.

Calibrate your tone of voice on paper to avoid sounding rushed, desperate, conflicted, unsure, or self-reproachful. Don't beat around the bush.

Don't write in the heat of the moment. Most things that seem overwhelming today will sort themselves out into manageable tasks by tomorrow. Instead of just dumping your big tangled issue into someone else's lap, break it into smaller problems that she can understand and solve.

While you work on framing your own needs, never let yourself lose sight of the other person's rights. If you need help to get out of a situation that's your fault, first admit it. Your need is not an entitlement and her willingness to help is not a blank check. Double that caution for relatives. Write a letter that puts your request in the best light, so that whether she can say yes or must say no, your friendship or family tie will still survive and thrive.

Don't add to your request for help a promise of what you are going to do in return, quid pro quo; your gratitude is your coin of payment. You will thank her in person; a little later, you will thank her on paper; and much later, you will do something for her in return. You don't have to preview your civility if your letter already minds its manners.

The desperation of a last-minute emergency request puts unfair pressure on the person you ask, and it casts doubt on how important the request actually is. The earlier you can let people know about your needs, the more enjoyable it is for them to help you.

MAKE IT PERSONAL

The materials that you choose for letters of request should be as simple, straightforward, and easy to read as your words. Handwritten letters work best for personal appeals.

Avoid any hint that this is a multiple request, making her feel like one of a crowd rather than someone who is valuable and unique.

If your letter is to be more formal (for instance, to ask for a letter of recommendation), select high-quality paper that conveys a more serious tone. Use a printout letter when you ask for career help, to show that you are organized and businesslike.

THE PREQUEST

If you are unsure about whether to ask for help at all, you can explore the matter with a short e-mail "elevator pitch," describing in a sentence or two what you would like to ask for. That way, you save everyone a bit of time and trouble if this is not the right favor, the right person, or the right time to ask. A longer letter either printed out or written by hand can follow if the answer is yes.

November 15, 2009

Dear Mitsuko,

It's been a long time since we've seen you. I hope you're well and that the garden is as green as we remember it from two years ago.

Graham and I will be coming to Los Angeles with the girls and wondered if we can take you up on that generous offer to come stay at your house. We arrive the 14th of January and go to San Diego the 17th. Mary and Sheila remember your stories with nostalgia and your pool with ferocious enthusiasm.

Sheila is participating in a gymnastics competition there. We've been immersed in her meets for the last six weeks here, and she just won honorable mention. I'm enclosing a snap of her in midair above the mat.

If it's not convenient for us to visit, let me know, and maybe we can still take you to "Leo's" and catch up over that famous chicken salad. We'll want to tell you about our travels and hear about yours.

Fondly,
Clarissa

CHOOSING THE RIGHT WORDS

- Don't camouflage your request as an innocent "How have you been?" letter that you've just happened to write. Open your letter with "I'm writing to ask for your help" or "I need your advice and help." Put the topic (your request) in the opening paragraph, or put "A request for your help" in the e-mail subject box.

- Be specific rather than opportunistic. For instance, rather than ask your friend in Washington, "Do you know anyone important who could help me get a job?," do your homework first and then zero in with, "I spoke with Mathilda Matterson, who manages the symphony gift shop. Since you know her, too, could you put in a good word for me?" Then supply some specifics to help her know what to say on your behalf and to whom.

- Offer a moderate serving of gratitude in advance. Describe the kindness of her actions rather than using overblown words of praise for her character. Gracefully express your debt without describing it as

---

Knowing that people sometimes can't come through with the hospitality they've offered, the young couple writing this letter ask about taking up the hostess on her standing invitation to "please come visit me again," while they leave the door open to several ways for her to respond.

part of a transaction that you plan to pay off. Write about "gratitude" rather than promising to "pay you back."

- Don't use awkward phrases such as "Thanking you in advance" and "What would I do without you?"
- Thank her for reading, and close with warmth.

CHAPTER 19

Fund-raising Letters

He who would use a friendship for profit
would cut down a flowering tree for firewood.

—George Washington

ife holds many opportunities to support your friends, your family, and the groups you believe in. Beyond offering them your own time, money, and effort, you can also contribute your connections, putting them in touch with other people who can help them. A personal letter often frames these requests that you make for help on someone else's behalf. You are probably almost too familiar with the letter from the friend inviting you to a fund-raiser, the request from a neighbor canvassing for a candidate, or the form letter seeking your pledge of dollars per mile for a colleague's walkathon. A letter, unlike a request in person, offers the potential giver time to think it over.

Whether you welcome these letters that contain secondhand requests or fend them off as blackmail, you may someday find yourself in the position of having to write one. "Please help my friend Jane" calls for a different letter from "Please help me." Give your appeal the best chance for success by your choice of format, and then find materials and words to suit the occasion.

RULES OF THUMB FOR WRITING A FUND-RAISING LETTER

You should send a fund-raising letter only on behalf of a person (or group) you are directly involved with, whom you already put effort and money of your own into supporting, and whom the potential donor might have some meaningful connection with.

The request to help someone else can have great benefits but also carries great risks. Exploiting the personal letter to raise money drains the personal element out of your friendships by making you play the role of either hustler or moneybags. If you are going to ask friends to donate to an organization, be upfront about your motives.

It's better to invite one friend at a time to support your cause, rather than canvass a big group. People like to feel special. Consider your reader's feelings and resources when you write. Don't ask an atheist to support your church, or a single mom just scraping by to host an expensive dinner. Don't solicit the same list of friends more than once a year.

Experienced development professionals learn not to cause "compassion fatigue" even in their most loyal supporters by asking too often. A proverb from many countries says, "The pitcher that goes to the well too often gets broken at last." Likewise, if you've asked someone for a contribution to an annual event, and the donor hasn't gotten interested in the organization, approach him carefully, only one more time. If you've asked twice and he hasn't donated, stop asking.

Also consider that when you write a request on behalf of someone else, your letter brings a third party, and his needs, into what was formerly a two-person relationship. Keep that factor in mind as you write.

At the beginning of your letter, describe the mission, scope, other supporters, and progress of the project. Describe what's needed for the recipient and from the donor. Offer a menu of options for contributing: money, attendance, membership, advice, time, effort, connections, donations in kind, or just being on the mailing list. Tell how the donation will benefit the recipient. Be specific. Cite your own level of commitment. Mention premiums, free tickets, reception, and other tokens of gratitude that the recipient offers.

Forecast whether this is a regular or a onetime need. If your group needs ongoing support, ask the person you are writing if you can put him on its mailing list, so that he begins to connect directly with the group rather than exclusively through you.

Also, be clear about whether this contribution is tax-deductible. Mention any matching funds.

You can make it easy to respond by including a specific request for action, a target date, full contact information, and a return envelope if appropriate. And you should establish reciprocity, so that the reader may feel free to solicit help from you for his projects in turn.

Sign by hand, with a warm closing, and handwrite the envelope. Use a stamp, not a postage machine.

Finally, before you send any request for help, start thinking about the letter of thanks that both you and the lucky recipient will owe the donor.

MAKE IT PERSONAL

Let your format, stationery, and wording give a clear indication of how special this request is and how much the cause means to you. Your choices will also give the reader a clue about how many other people you are asking to help. On the one hand, an impersonal e-mail with forty-nine names showing in the "address" box announces that you are asking everyone you know. On the other hand, if you are frank about its wide distribution, no one will think that you are camouflaging the nature of your letter.

If you don't want your recipient to feel like just a name on a list, tailor your letter to him personally. A letter written in longhand on personal-size stationery implies that this person is the only one, or one of very few, you're asking. Let the reader know how important his help is without letting desperation creep in. Use dignified, high-quality materials and your own handwriting. You can enclose, or follow up with, a small amount of explanatory material.

A printout letter works best when you are asking for help for a group, since it conveys a semiformal institutional tone and weight. It also lets you quickly give a lot of repetitive detail. Write a personal salutation, and sign each letter by hand. Hand-address the envelope and add your name to any return-address imprint.

CHOOSING THE RIGHT WORDS

- Include a personal salutation. Even a handwritten letter can start with a group affiliation, such as "Dear Fellow Tuba Lover" when you are seeking support for a friend's performance. This lets your reader know he has been chosen for a special reason, and that you are mailing to only a few people like him.

- Be sure you include three elements: narrate the story, describe your involvement, and acknowledge any help you've already received—even if it is only a request for information. Try to find a way to use the

Dear Margaret,   4-12-08
I just wanted to thank you again
for putting me in touch with Zöe
Friend, and to share with you her
marvelous design for the t-shirts
we're printing for children at
the Airfield School in Ghana.

What a success! Zöe
so beautifully
captured the
idea of being
"lifted up" by
education, and
the hope it gives
to these children.

Education Gives Me Wings!
HO AIRFIELD SCHOOL

To learn more about the new school
we're building for them, go to
www.pagusafrica.org. You'll see
that they need everything - from
pencils and glue sticks, to
financial donations in any
amount.
Thanks again for all your support
and encouragement.
                                    Annie

phrase "you helped" or "you can help" rather than "we need," if possible.

- Express your own commitment to the cause and relate it to the possibility of a shared new interest for the two of you. Rather than say, "It will mean a lot to me," use specific details, such as "I have visited this village myself twice and admire the clinic staff's devotion. It would remind you of the clinic you saw in Thailand," or "I hope that you can attend the opening so that you can see the work of the art class I volunteer for." Offer the reader a chance to participate in your activities.
- On printout letters, add marginal notes by hand, such as "I really enjoy these gallery talks and hope you'll join us for one," or "One of these doctors teaches at the same hospital where you were a candy striper."

Asking for help on behalf of others is not just about collecting money but about nurturing connections. In this letter, the writer thanks the reader for providing a professional contact, describes a project, and shows her what her help has already created, while graciously asking for her interest, useful items, and money. The handwriting makes this letter intensely personal, while the new logo adds an image of the project.

CHAPTER 20

Letters of Conscience

> *Never doubt that a small group of thoughtful,*
> *committed people can change the world.*
> *Indeed, it is the only thing that ever has.*
>
> —*Anthropologist Margaret Mead (1901–1978)*

The art of the personal letter includes writing about something very important to you to someone in a position of authority, who usually doesn't know you personally. The letter to the editor about the other side of a story, the request to your local state representative to resist budget cuts, the plea to your college administration about academic policies, the complaint to the head of a corporation about toxic products—all are part of your privilege and duty as a citizen.

Any personal letter lets you speak your mind, but a letter prompted by conscience can let your voice serve as a powerful moral tool for social change. When you decide to speak truth to power, paying attention to how you write it will ensure that your voice is heard.

RULES OF THUMB FOR WRITING A
LETTER OF CONSCIENCE

You need a good reason to write to someone who does not know you: You see injustice and want to speak out, you want to register your opinion, or you feel that your side of a debate has not been aired. Just being angry, or wanting something, is not enough to ensure that your ideas will be recognized.

Whatever prompts you to write, don't waste the reader's time by venting your frustration. Write with passion, but edit with reason. Write calmly and logically. A letter of conscience puts you up on a soapbox already. Don't rant.

State your main point immediately, and be accurate. You can put the topic in a headline above the salutation to help the reader grasp your subject. If more than one person will sign the letter, identify the common concern of everyone in the group, and then describe what action you would like the reader to take.

Stay on topic. Don't start out about local school lunches and end up making an antiwar protest.

In addition, avoid personal attacks. Write about a problem that you believe should and can be solved, not about the person you think is causing it.

You must include your name, street address, and phone number. Editors at newspapers and magazines are on guard about fake identities and will usually contact you to verify

June 25, 2007

Mr. President,

   As members of the Presidential
Scholars class of 2007, we have
been told that we represent the
best and brightest of our nation.
Therefore, we believe we have a
responsibility to voice our convictions.
   We do not want America to
represent torture. We urge you to
do all in your power to stop
violations of the human rights
of detainees, to cease illegal renditions,
and to apply the Geneva Convention
to all detainees, including those
designated enemy combatants.

                    Signed,

Mari Oye   Colin McSwiggen
Mari Oye, MA   Colin McSwiggen, OH

that you actually wrote your letter. Anonymous letters lack credibility.

Before sending your letter, sleep on it. Revise it. Ask someone to review it to make sure that your writing is clear and that you are getting your point across.

A writer at the Community ToolBox Web site advises, "Be quick, be concise, and then be quiet." Make one letter count. Don't keep mailing additional versions of the same message.

MAKE IT PERSONAL

Your letter will persuade best when it comes from the heart. Write sincerely about what is important to you, not to someone else, using your own, not someone else's words. Editors have learned to steer clear of what they call "Astroturf"—letters that appear to come from the grass roots but are actually composed by a special-interest group. A newspaper op-ed page editor in Syracuse, New York, advises, "We want to publish letters that are composed by local writ-

---

Two high-school seniors, who were part of a group of other Presidential Scholars, drafted a letter of protest againt torture, collected fifty signatures from their fellow honorees, and presented it in person to George Bush at a 2007 White House reception. This dramatic letter of conscience brought their cause to the attention of the news media, whether it changed the president's mind or not.

ers, in their own words, not copied from some boilerplate concocted by some lobbyist or public relations flack."

E-mail works especially well for time-sensitive letters about fast-changing current topics (like letters to the editor). Although most newspaper and magazine editors prefer e-mail, because the text usually doesn't have to be retyped for publication, they don't object to handwritten letters; it just takes longer to process them. Handwriting shows authenticity. A handwritten letter emphasizes that your voice is that of an individual, rather than that of a group. A letter written by a child shows unmatched sincerity and autonomy.

Letters printed out on business-size stationery allow you to send signed copies to local media easily. More than one person can sign this type of letter, too, although using an organization's letterhead will overshadow your voice as an individual. Your letter also can be sent to more than one person; for example, an open letter to a college dean may be distributed and publicized to related organizations on campus.

Suit your method of delivery to the occasion. Telephone the switchboard or check the Web site to identify the person you should write to. When in doubt, take it to the top—the president, CEO, or chair. When you write to a corporation or the government, don't immediately send copies to the media until you have explored other avenues and your attempts have failed. Keep a record of what you have written. Register delivery if you think proof is needed. Dramatize the letter's delivery if you think that handing it directly to a person in public will help your cause.

CHOOSING THE RIGHT WORDS

- Include a call to action that describes what you hope to see happen, and also mention what may ensue if nothing happens. For example, "The school day starts too early, and the starting time must change. High-school students need their rest. If they get too little sleep, they will not perform well in school or learn their lessons."
- To establish your expertise, add your title after your signature: M.D., Ph.D., Rev., Capt., or Esq. Use Ms., Mrs., Miss, or Mr. to identify your gender.
- Include your age or status if it adds to your message. A fourth grader can testify to the next generation's fears about global warming, whereas an eighty-six-year-old offers unique insight into veteran's benefits.
- Don't say "I feel" or "My feeling is." The facts and the possible solutions to a problem are more important than your feelings. Even "I think," "In my opinion," or "I believe" dilutes your message.

WRITING A LETTER TO THE EDITOR

Before writing a letter to the editor, review the newspaper or magazine's policy on letter length and submission guidelines. Keep your letter to fewer than 300 words to have it read, fewer than 200 words to have it published, and fewer than 140 words to have it published more quickly. The average length of letters printed in national newsmagazines is about eighty words. Many papers also limit publication to one letter per month per writer.

CHAPTER 21

Letters of Thanks

Sin is anything less than the occasion requires.
—*Walter Kerr*, The Decline of Pleasure, 1962

How do you put your feelings into words when someone does something extra special for you? Although
a quick thank-you note may be enough for a home-cooked
dinner or a housewarming gift, what can you do to express
major gratitude to people who have helped your career with
a glowing recommendation, bestowed a gift that you treasure, galloped to your rescue, or opened their doors to your
whole family with over-the-top hospitality?

You may already have said thank you in person, or sent
your gratitude by e-mail, or mailed a short handwritten
note. But somehow your effort still doesn't seem equal to
what he did for you, and you still have that nagging feeling that he doesn't really know how grateful you feel. For
you, even more than for the person you are indebted to,
nothing feels more dismal than underthanking and noth-

ing feels more virtuous than sending a letter of genuine thanks.

A thank-you letter is not just longer than a thank-you note but also philosophically broader, signaling that you are aware of how blessed you are, and putting the whole matter on permanent record. E-mail is far too offhand, and even a traditional handwritten note doesn't commemorate significant help the way a longer handwritten letter does. Writing by hand acknowledges that something important, above the ordinary, exists between the two of you. Personal letters show that you know you are part of a relationship that is strong enough to sustain large gifts, efforts, career help, and hospitality, and that you are doing your part by being grateful, on paper.

You might also write a thank-you letter for a series of sustained small efforts. For example, if a friend has given you a ride to choir practice every week all year, you could of course thank him with a small gift or an offer to pay for gas; a letter, however, will express the gratitude you feel for the kind of effort that can't be repaid with merchandise or money. He picked you up out of kindness and friendship, not to earn gas money or a car-wash coupon.

Finally, it's almost never too late to *rethank* someone. During the chaos of a wedding, for instance, many details inevitably get overlooked. You may discover that you have completely missed thanking someone for a gift or favor. And while every gift is special, some are more special than others. Although you may have written a good-enough thank-you note to your maid of honor at the time, later you can write a personal letter to thank her for her weeks of work and days of devotion. Your belated thank-you letter, if you don't load it with melodramatic excuses, can make up in length for what it lacks in punctuality.

A letter of gratitude also keeps the channels open for more help in the future. Living far from your family at college, you can satisfy both your little brother and your conscience by taking a quarter of an hour in October to write him a letter about how much you love waking up every day to the music of the clock radio he bought for you in late August.

Whether you have been blessed with a substantial gift, a stream of smaller gifts, career help, or simply the patience of someone who deserves more thanks than you have already sent, you can write a letter that puts you in the state of grace that comes only from having properly thanked someone who truly deserves it.

RULES OF THUMB FOR WRITING A THANK-YOU LETTER

Start off by mentioning the gift by name, and describe how you benefited. Give details about the gift he gave or the reward he helped you get.

1:00 AM

Dear Lindsay,

Have I ever told you what a great roommate you are? I come home from the absolute <u>worst day</u> at the clinic and there's a six pack and a pepperoni pizza. You must have read my mind, and not for the first time either!

It reminded me of that New Yorker cartoon where the guy coming home from work sees a martini extended out the front door on a ten-foot pole to greet him. You made me feel better before I even hung up my coat. I owe you one.

Keep doing what you're doing.

Gavin

Acknowledge your indebtedness but don't exaggerate. Be lavish but not melodramatic. Psychologists talk about the "tyranny of the gift," when the recipient can't ever be grateful enough; there's also a similar "tyranny of the thank-you," when the gratitude is inflated out of proportion to the giver's intentions. The reader will be most interested in your gratitude, not your unworthiness or your lateness.

Add details about your own life, plus news, plans, and opinions. Then allude to your ongoing connection with the reader, and close with warmth.

MAKE IT PERSONAL

If your gratitude is worth a letter, it's worth a good-looking letter. Choose materials that are either fine and formal or warm and cozy, depending on the nature of your letter. Avoid arty and idiosyncratic paper or comic note cards. Use white or off-white unlined paper that is slightly smaller than standard business stationery. Don't write a personal letter on your employer's stationery or stamp it through the postage machine! Print it out in pleasantly readable black type, or handwrite it with black, blue, or blue-black ink.

One roommate writes to another with the sort of appreciation that could have been expressed aloud but which packs an extra punch on paper.

Your materials should be age-appropriate for both you and your reader. Well-chosen paper and ink can show respect to your elders, speak the language of your peers, or catch the fancy of the small fry.

For a lasting monument to gratitude, use ink on good stationery. Even the best e-mail suggests you are cutting corners for your own convenience. E-mail is too offhand, and a printout letter is often too impersonal, for a task that demands evidence of sincerity and effort.

Do, however, send a printout letter when you thank a friend who has gone to bat professionally by writing a letter of recommendation for you.

THANKS FOR THE THANKS

Take care when sending a thank-you for a thank-you. If you were blown away by a thank-you note or hostess gift from someone expressing his own gratitude, don't trump him with an elaborate "You're welcome" note, which may make him feel like he's back where he started—in debt again. Practice one-downmanship. Respond to a thank-you gift with a short note, if you feel grateful, and to a handwritten thank-you note with a brief e-mail or a verbal reply. That lets the thanker continue to feel that his gratitude is appropriately received, not bounced back again to require yet more thanks.

Most personal letters rest on the assumption of an ongoing connection. If you are writing to thank a person (such as an interviewer) for simply doing his job, send a short business note, not a long personal letter about yourself and your dreams.

CHOOSING THE RIGHT WORDS

- Say thank you on paper with many of the same words you would use in person if you could have an hour over a cup of tea or coffee to talk and catch up. Use words like *grateful, kind, glad, thanks, thank you, thankful,* and *appreciate.*
- Praise the reader's kindness specifically. Write "You are so thoughtful!" or "You made me feel so welcome," rather than "You are such a great person" or "That was a wonderful present."
- Share your delight and acknowledge the giver's role in making something possible for you: "Thanks to you and your letter of recommendation, I got hired right away—only six days of nail biting and stewing. Then they needed me the next day. I am already finding that the skills I learned from watching you with a classroom full of four-year-olds are very useful when I deal with fourteen-year-olds."

January 21, 2009

Dear Grandma,

Dan and I will celebrate our first anniversary next Wednesday, and I want to let you know that when we defrost and cut the square of wedding cake we will be using your beautiful silver server.

I remember it from your big house on B Avenue, when you used to hold afternoon tea and we watched you and your friends talk grown-up talk. It has turned out to be our family heirloom already; we not only treasure it but use it. It's beautiful and it reminds us of you. I'm happy to have an initial that matches the scrolly *A* on the handle.

We were so grateful you could make the long trip to come to the wedding. It meant so much to us. I hope you've enjoyed the album we sent. I wanted to be sure you realize what an important part of the celebration you were.

I hope you're well.

Much love,
Athena

- Write "I hope I can help someone else the way you have helped me" or "Thank you from the bottom of my heart," rather than an obvious exaggeration such as "You've saved my life" or "I owe you my firstborn."

This letter follows an earlier, shorter note, not just to remind an elderly relative of gratitude for a gift but also to share a happy memory with her. Although this would be sent as an attachment—if Grandma uses e-mail—by arriving in an envelope it lets her enjoy the old-fashioned elegance of a letter while benefiting from the readability of large type.

CHAPTER 22

Letters of Apology

*One of the hardest things in this world is to
admit you are wrong. And nothing is more helpful in
resolving a situation than its frank admission.*

—Benjamin Disraeli (1804–1881)

*E*veryone blunders once in a while, through not caring or not planning or not paying enough attention. Making mistakes is a universal human weakness. Whether you've said it, done it, or written it (or simply forgotten to do one of these), occasionally you make a mistake that causes trouble for someone you care about. You shouldn't add insult to injury by neglecting to apologize. From a child confessing her misdeeds to God or a drunk apologizing to a hostess on the morning after a binge, to a former U.S. secretary of defense apologizing for the Vietnam War, the acknowledgment of wrongdoing is one of the most powerful human actions.

You can transform weakness to strength by apologizing in one of the best ways possible—on paper. A well-written letter can help you repair the connection between you and the person you've just injured, insulted, offended, annoyed, or inconvenienced.

Let's face it, though: Goofing up feels just terrible. It's hard to say you're sorry. You sit down to write, carrying an awkward load of mingled guilt, shame, humiliation, regret, embarrassment, resentment, and plain old cowardice. You may be tempted just to wait for it to blow over. You may persuade yourself that maybe no one noticed. Nevertheless, it doesn't matter that you may be feeling worse than the person you have hurt. It doesn't matter if you meant to do something hurtful or not. You have to get over it. The best way out of this mess is through the kind of care and effort that you can make visible with your words on paper. Whether you blurted out the name of your niece's secret crush, missed someone else's deadline, crashed your boss's laptop, or blew your cool at a party, you can still write the kind of apology that will help to heal your relationship with the other person.

RULES OF THUMB FOR WRITING A LETTER OF APOLOGY

Greet the reader with courtesy, and thank her for reading your letter. Then clearly name the injury. Don't be vague about what happened. A letter of apology begins with a mea culpa—literally, "I am to blame." Don't start until you are ready to admit just that; no protests, no self-defense, no ex-

---

A CAUTION FOR APOLOGIES

If you have harmed someone materially—that is, caused a personal injury or property damage—consult a lawyer before you put your admission of guilt into writing.

---

planations. Do not try to blame the reader or some third person for what you did.

Don't exaggerate. That just makes you important. If you misspelled someone's name on an award, it's not the end of the world and you're not a miserable sinner; you just made a mistake that can be apologized for and corrected. Remember that a proper apology is always about the injured party.

Choose warm, soft, gentle words. As G. K. Chesterton said, "A stiff apology is a second insult. . . . The injured party does not want to be compensated because he has been wronged; he wants to be healed because he has been hurt."

Acknowledge your responsibility and express your regret. Be apologetic but don't grovel.

Do not take her forgiveness for granted. Ask, but don't demand, to be forgiven.

Promise that the error will not happen again, and offer restitution. If you broke something, offer to pay for replacing it.

As you close, offer gratitude for the other person's tolerance, and express best wishes for the relationship to survive your blunder.

MAKE IT PERSONAL

Entrepreneurs have tried to cash in on the cowardly side of human nature by selling "e-pology" items—apology e-cards, apology certificates, apology teddy bears, or apology bouquets—to people who just can't bring themselves to write a letter. These Web sites offer prefab apologies—and even condolences—with such come-ons as "Sorry seems to be the hardest word. . . . Not anymore!" and "Show the world your apology. . . . Have it placed in the scrolling site Marquis" and "I'm Sorry.com offers three easy, effective ways of apologizing. Every option works!" These slapdash apologies just make the situation worse. If you have caused trouble, you must take trouble in order to show that you are seriously sorry.

A recent study by whitepages.com found that 80 percent of persons polled described e-mail as being easy to misinterpret. Not only is the e-mail tone of voice intrinsically harsh, but people may be offended simply by your choice of this low-effort format. To be sure your regret sounds sincere, use e-mail to apologize only for the most trivial gaffes, such as botching an introduction. E-mail is appropriate when

Sunday March 5, 2000

Dear CJ,

Thanks so much for taking me out last Tuesday. It's always so nice to see you and catch up on your life, and what the group is doing. It's hard to believe that 2 years has gone by since we started this tradition.

I was way out of line, though, when I told you what I thought of Nancy's roommate. I hope you'll accept my apology. I don't know what I was thinking or why I thought it was any of my business. Sometimes my mouth just keeps going - long after my brain has left the scene.

I really did enjoy meeting the girls. You were so generous to take everyone out for pizza. I'm hoping next time we can meet at my house.

All the best -

Georgia

you shouldn't blow little goofs out of proportion with huge apologies.

E-mail does, however, let you start to handle an enormous mistake by asking immediately if you may apologize in person. Between these two extremes, however, don't apologize by e-mail.

For most medium-size mistakes, write a handwritten letter with the goal of having a face-to-face conversation, the way most people prefer, as soon as possible. Your paper and ink colors should be simple and subdued but not stark. Stay away from legalistic black-and-white printout letters on business stationery.

CHOOSING THE RIGHT WORDS

- Don't say "Mistakes were made," "I apologize for anything I might have done," "I may have offended you," "I'm sorry you feel this way," "Whatever I did," "I'm so stupid," "You must be so mad," "You must hate me," "I was just kidding," "I SAID I was sorry; what more do you want?," or "Can't you take a joke?"

A woman writes to apologize for sticking her foot in her mouth. She keeps the focus on the first and last paragraphs on what her friend did right, preventing her own gaffe from diminishing her friend's efforts.

- Do say "I was responsible for that; it's my fault" or "I have no excuse. It won't happen again."
- Never use the word *but*. To write "I am sorry, but" implies that you are not actually sorry.
- Use words such as *sorry, regret, apology, repent, amend, offense, injury, forgive,* and *pardon.*
- Now is the time to describe your gratitude for the relationship, using names and nouns. Let your reader know how much she means to you. Refer to "my forgiving friend," "my long-suffering mom," or "my patient husband," and close with "your very sorry niece," or "From an apologetic, grateful friend."

CHAPTER 23

Letters to the Future

*Letters are the most significant memorial
a person can leave behind.*

—Johann Wolfgang von Goethe (1749–1832)

*N*othing brings someone from the past back to life more convincingly than a letter. The handwriting, the language, and even the choice of paper combine to let a voice speak again in our mind. I recently bought a little jewelry box at a flea market, and in dusting off one of the drawers, I found a paper from its previous owner—a will that specified which music to play at her funeral, what she was to be dressed in, and who was to receive each of her possessions. It was signed, "Louisa, age 9." Writing on mint green paper bordered with little footprints and bugs, she almost felt like someone I knew.

The words that pass through your pen or your keyboard can make you vividly real long after you write them: to your future self, to the adult your child will become, or to someone you don't know yet. You expand your world today just by writing such a letter. With a little planning and luck, you may reach someone in a tomorrow you can only imagine.

You can draft an heirloom letter on a happy or a sad occasion. Starting college or graduating, expecting a baby, turning forty, facing surgery or preparing for battle, accepting a bad diagnosis or a fatal prognosis—each may prompt you to pen a sharply focused view of your life and its meaning. Sometimes writing down your thoughts about timeless issues can feel much easier than speaking them out loud amid the chatter of daily life. It's energizing to write about serious topics today if you know that the coming years will add depth to your words for someone you love.

A letter written to someone in a time to come is different from a journal entry in which you talk to your future self. A legacy letter challenges your imagination to conjure up not only a person perhaps as yet unknown or even unborn and the relationship between you but also the words you want to say when that person sits down to read. In fact, this letter may *be* the entire relationship, the only way the person will ever know your voice. The format, the words, and even the materials you choose take on new importance.

You can write several types of letters to someone in the future—to yourself, or to new baby, or a kind of message in a bottle "to whom it may concern" that has something to say to whoever finds it. This chapter will focus on writing to your own child or younger relative; this is the most typical kind of letter to the future, and the most poignant.

Your child is always in the process of becoming some-one. From the hopeful rose-colored dreams you give words to in the weeks before his arrival, to the letter you write to him fourteen years later instead of biting his head off, to the first letter you send him in his own apartment, your child will eventually treasure any words that give him insight into his origins and early years. Some parents make a custom of writing an annual birthday letter, with its dual focus on the past and the future, and they put away an extra copy. Your ongoing perspective on your child's life, while it may not ever jibe with his own inner picture, will eventually help him triangulate on where he comes from and who he is.

Increasingly referred to as the "dying letter," "keepsake letter," "heirloom letter," or "legacy letter," this kind of writing made headlines in the 2008 presidential primary when Elizabeth Edwards, the wife of Senator John Edwards and a cancer patient, spoke frankly of her ongoing project to put her thoughts and dreams on paper for her family: "You don't know when your time's going to come and whether you're going to have any warning, and it would be a great idea to pass on the things you thought would be important to them." She wrote her three children a good-bye letter in which she talked to them about life, how to choose a church, and marriage. She added, ". . . it just tells them the things I hope that they'll know about growing up. I know they'd have their father as a great moral guide, but of course, there's no mother who doesn't want to get her two cents in."

Equal parts journal and postcard, candid snapshot and studio portrait, and a blend of thank you, apology, advice, and love, this kind of letter can draw a picture that lasts.

RULES OF THUMB FOR WRITING A LETTER TO THE FUTURE

Your letter to the future requires some simple planning so that it can survive and thrive. Write it in a format that will last and continue to be easy to read. Date your letter, and explain who and where you are.

The perspective of your heirloom letter should include the inner landscape of your mind as well as a glimpse of the world around you. Clarity and detail sharpen the focus nearby, while a sense of purpose extends the far horizon. Don't bother with an overview of vague generalities that everyone knows ("Honor your heritage" or "Do unto others") or dwell on trivia like weather, politics, squabbles, and minor illnesses. Instead, write about a few specific, even quirky, things that you value most. Search for the telling detail, things that can link you to the other person's world, such as how you are reminded of your own mother's hands whenever you slice the Sabbath challah on her bread dish, how you met your spouse, or how you planted a special tree for your child in the garden of your first house.

If you have a terminal illness, you have some especially

important legacy letters to write. You have to get past some very normal first impulses—to detail the miseries of the illness itself, to focus on your sorrow at leaving your family, to pity those left behind, and to pour all of life's wisdom into a few pages. These thoughts belong more appropriately in a journal. Instead, write about how happy you are about having your family, how much you love them, how strong you hope they will be, how much help you anticipate will come from others around them, and how much wisdom they will gain. They will have a lot to cope with; don't add your pain to theirs but, rather, use your letter to give them emotional support. Several letters from you addressed to them at specific milestones in the future—at age twelve, say, or on the occasion of their marriage, or on the arrival of a new baby—will help them refresh the picture in their minds of you at their own age, rather than remembering you only at the age you had reached when you left them.

Include your dreams as well as your philosophies; these gain poignancy—and sometimes unexpected humor—with the passing of time. If you let your son imagine your life before he came and what a good difference he made, someday he'll be able to put himself in your shoes. If you just preach windy, generalized advice at him, he may shrug it off.

Give your letter a positive spin. Write about the things that make him special—not about how much you worried when he broke his arm, but about how brave the doctor told him he was; not about how cute he was, but how beloved.

Detail the beginnings of things he may not remember—
the decisions that led to the move he hated in second grade,
how much someone he may only dimly remember doted
on him, the well-wishers at last-year's birthday, or an overheard compliment you never passed along. Showcase small
insights that only you know about. Reading that "Grandpa
Geoff would have loved watching you learn to split a log,"
and why, may fill a little of that empty space if your child
was born after his grandfather died.

Finally, however you plan to archive your letter and its
keepsakes, label it and its purpose clearly: "For Estelle at
age twenty-one" or "To Thomas, before his first date," or
"To myself, at fifty," or "This letter goes with Grandma's
pearl necklace," or "In the event of my death." Although it's
charming to rely on future serendipity, it's better to make
sure your priceless letter will actually be discovered. Tell
someone else now where it can be found.

MAKE IT PERSONAL

The twentieth century, littered with many bright ideas for
sending and saving words, has seen most of these inventions
become obsolete while ink on paper has endured. The Edi-
son cylinder, the Dictaphone, the long-playing record, the
reel-to-reel tape, and the eight-track tape have all had their

day. Similarly, people have tried to make their words permanent with many generations of microfilm, microfiche, optical disks, floppy disks, and hard disks. Most of these storage platforms would be very difficult to read today and impossible to read a generation from now. Computer files in early computer languages, too, have all lapsed into a state of mute unreadability. Even paper was not safe from meddling; a brief archival fad for encasing paper in solid acrylic slabs ruined many documents in the 1970s.

Your letter will survive better if you resist the latest high-tech format and rely instead on the time-tested medium of permanent ink on high-quality paper, stored with care. Write in your own handwriting if you can, to make your presence most vivid, though the typography of the era can also convey a period flavor to future generations. On the eve of a long trip in 1956 to join my father, who was ill on the other side of the world, my mother left a "just in case" letter in her files for her little girls. The old Elite type with the off-kilter *M* transports me back to her study just as vividly as her words of closing, "God bless you. I can only wish you as happy a life as I have had; as fine a husband or wife, as rich experiences, as much fun." I knew nothing of this serene and purposeful letter until ten years after her death, when a carbon copy turned up in some old legal papers.

Choose paper for durability. Although you can go first-class with archival thesis paper designed for Ph.D. disserta-

December 20, 1989

Dear Sophie,

One week ago your mother and father
called me in the middle of the night to tell me
about the safe arrival of the baby they wanted
for so long— you! Today I got to meet you, my
first granddaughter. They dressed you in a
bright red suit with mistletoe embroidered on
the hood, and carried you up to the big green
door of my house past mountains of snowdrifts.

It will be fun to watch you grow up. I plan
to tell you stories about your grandmother, whose
smile looked so much like yours. Her name was
Sophia, too, and she loved practical jokes, the
color red, and the view from the orchard. When
you are 4 years old you can try and climb the

apple tree she planted when she lived here.
Maybe you'll make apple pies someday too!

When your dad was a little boy in this
house, he used to sneak down the back stairs &
munch his way through the kitchen cabinets
before sunrise. He was too short to reach the
chocolate chips, so he dragged the stepladder in
from the garage—he was the hungriest kid I
ever knew. I hope you'll grow up to be as
curious and funny as your father and as kind
and gentle as your mother. Jokes are good but
hugs are even better, when people need a smile.

Enjoy every day. Remember, wherever
I am, I'll be thinking about you.
                    Love, Grandpa Max

STORING AN HEIRLOOM LETTER

How you store your letter to the future, or your treasured heirloom letters from others, is just as important as what it is made of. Archival paper won't resist yellowing if it spends a decade in a plain manila file folder inside a corrugated cardboard box. Even a simple stationery envelope, or a sandwich of two blank stationery sheets, will offer some protection. Don't sleeve your letter in plastic, which will trap moisture, nor laminate it, which is irreversible.

If you intend to include a keepsake such as a recording, a photograph, or a lock of hair, reference it in the letter, wrap it separately, and pad the whole package to keep the letter paper flat and unstained. Never staple, paper-clip, or tape anything to your letter. If you include a newspaper clipping, wrap it separately to prevent it from staining your letter as the newsprint yellows, or photocopy it onto better paper and store that. Keep any valuable letter away from moisture, heat, dirt, bugs, or mice and from the direct light of the sun, a lamp, or a photocopier. If you want to display a treasured letter, frame it behind UV glass on archival matte board to keep the ink from fading and the paper from yellowing, and hang it out of the sun.

On the preceding two pages, an elderly man writes fondly and vividly to his newborn granddaughter, offering her his own memories of the grandmother she will never meet, vignettes of his son as a little boy, and tales of her first visit to his house. He writes of past, present, and future family scenes, to draw for her a picture slowly flowing by. This letter can speak to her soon, when she is a little girl, but also later when she has become a grown woman.

tions, even good-quality stationery with a high rag content will last much longer than standard wood-pulp printer paper.

CHOOSING THE RIGHT WORDS

- The words you choose can comfort and energize your reader years later, or they can distress and demoralize him. Use your pen to draw a portrait of what you believe and hope, not what you mourn and fear. Choose phrases such as: "I hope," "I trust," "I'm sure," "I believe," "I know," "I wonder," "I enjoyed," "I loved," and words such as *gratitude, comfort, blessing, importance, happiness, joy, content, always, now, still, forever, memories,* and *future.*
- Use reassuring statements such as "My love will always be with you—you get to keep it with you and remember it forever."
- Lighten the uncertainty of the unknown with the strength of your connection with the reader and the comfort of the familiar: "I don't know what comes next, but I believe that what we keep in the imagination can't ever be taken from us. You and I have had so many chances to enjoy life."

- Use negative, unhappy words like *sorrow, sorry, sad, regret, separation, death, never,* and *unfair* sparingly or not at all.
- If the letter is written to one person, use his name several times throughout the letter. If you write to several children, take the time to rephrase your thoughts somewhat differently for each.

The more letters you read, the more ways you'll think of to write. And the more letters you write, the better you'll get at seeing fresh opportunities to stay in touch. Add this creative art to your life whenever you want to transform ordinary words into something special.

About the Authors

MARGARET SHEPHERD is a noted writer, calligrapher, and teacher. After writing more than a dozen books about learning calligraphy, she brought an artist's eye to her best-selling books about the art of handwritten notes and civilized conversation. *The Art of the Personal Letter* continues her advocacy for being in touch—with style—in the twenty-first century. She lives in Boston.

SHARON CLOUD HOGAN has written and edited several books for general readers. She leads workshops on nonfiction writing for physicians, and she is a manuscript editor at *The New England Journal of Medicine*. She lives near Boston.